CAPITAL ACCESS

SELECT RESEARCH ON FUNDING OF BUSINESSES OWNED BY WOMEN AND MINORITIES

BUSINESS ISSUES, COMPETITION AND ENTREPRENEURSHIP

Additional books in this series can be found on Nova's website
under the Series tab.

Additional E-books in this series can be found on Nova's website
under the E-book tab.

CAPITAL ACCESS

SELECT RESEARCH ON FUNDING OF BUSINESSES OWNED BY WOMEN AND MINORITIES

HOPE DREXLER

AND

GREGORY MAINES

EDITORS

nova publishers
New York

For permission to use material from this book please contact us:
Telephone 631-231-7269; Fax 631-231-8175
Web Site: http://www.novapublishers.com

NOTICE TO THE READER

The Publisher has taken reasonable care in the preparation of this book, but makes no expressed or implied warranty of any kind and assumes no responsibility for any errors or omissions. No liability is assumed for incidental or consequential damages in connection with or arising out of information contained in this book. The Publisher shall not be liable for any special, consequential, or exemplary damages resulting, in whole or in part, from the readers' use of, or reliance upon, this material. Any parts of this book based on government reports are so indicated and copyright is claimed for those parts to the extent applicable to compilations of such works.

Independent verification should be sought for any data, advice or recommendations contained in this book. In addition, no responsibility is assumed by the publisher for any injury and/or damage to persons or property arising from any methods, products, instructions, ideas or otherwise contained in this publication.

This publication is designed to provide accurate and authoritative information with regard to the subject matter covered herein. It is sold with the clear understanding that the Publisher is not engaged in rendering legal or any other professional services. If legal or any other expert assistance is required, the services of a competent person should be sought. FROM A DECLARATION OF PARTICIPANTS JOINTLY ADOPTED BY A COMMITTEE OF THE AMERICAN BAR ASSOCIATION AND A COMMITTEE OF PUBLISHERS.

Additional color graphics may be available in the e-book version of this book.

Library of Congress Cataloging-in-Publication Data

ISBN: 978-1-62948-197-5

Published by Nova Science Publishers, Inc. † New York

CONTENTS

PREFACE

Chapter 1 - This report examines access to capital by young and small businesses. The purpose of the investigation is to gain a better understanding of access to capital by young firms and how the recent economic and financial crisis has affected their access to financial capital, especially among firms owned by women and minorities and firms that are high tech in nature. In light of the key role in small business finance played by financial institutions, this study pays disproportionate attention to access to bank loans. Although these issues are important, research has traditionally been limited by a lack of appropriate data. A primary obstacle has been the absence of representative samples of small businesses that contain detailed descriptions of their access to financing. The primary source of data on this question, the Federal Reserve Survey of Small Business Finances, was discontinued in 2003, and is thus unavailable for studying the effects of the financial crisis on small businesses.

A second obstacle has been the tendency of researchers to analyze data on cross sections of small businesses of varying ages and sizes at a single point in time. While the findings from these snapshots have been valuable to scholars and policymakers, they have also been limited. Because they are static, these snapshots do not capture the ways in which small business financing unfolds over the life cycle of the firm and changes over time. This study attempts to overcome these obstacles by examining the effects of the changing financial environment generally and the economic crisis specifically, on access to capital by small businesses over the 2004 through 2010 period, controlling for business and owner characteristics. Analyses of small-firm capital access are based upon firm subsets drawn from the Kauffman Firm Survey.

Key findings of this study include the fact that firms owned by African Americans and Latinos utilize a different mix of equity and debt capital, relative to firms owned by nonminorities. Relying disproportionately upon owner equity investments and employing relatively less debt from outside sources (primarily banks), the average firm in these minority business subgroups operates with substantially less capital overall – both at startup and in subsequent years – relative to their nonminority counterparts. Women-owned businesses exhibit some similar disparities in capital structure, relative to male-owned firms, in the sense of operating with much less capital, on average, and a somewhat different mix of debt and equity capital. Their reliance upon outside equity capital is particularly low. The initial disparities in the levels of startup capital by business owner race, ethnicity, and gender do not disappear in the subsequent years following startup.

The information asymmetry inherent with new and young firms is exacerbated in high technology industries due to the lack of tangible assets and their reliance on knowledge assets, as well as technical and market uncertainty. The information asymmetries associated with new firms in general, and high tech firms specifically, make traditional bank lenders less likely to lend to these firms. This report also examines financing patters of high tech firms.

This study will help government officials document significant racial and gender disparities in capital access, differences in lending patterns between high tech and non-high tech firms, and credit market conditions during the financial crisis. These results will help policymakers in developing policies to ensure optimal access to debt and equity capital among all small businesses, including during times of financial stress.

Chapter 2 – Studies of Women-Led Businesses (WLBs) have increased dramatically over the past 15 years. One consistent finding in this research is that WLBs receive less outside funding than Men-Led Businesses (MLBs). Further, Venture Capital (VC) funding of WLBs consisted of only 6% of the total funds invested in the United States between 1997 and 2000. Are there unique features to the VC firms that invest in WLBs? And how does investing in WLBs affect the subsequent performance of VC firms? Our study addresses these questions using a social capital lens.

Our data for this study consist of all U.S. VC investments from 2000 through 2010. The dataset includes 2,500 VC firms, 18,900 portfolio companies (those companies VC firms invested in during the 11 year period of the study), 92,500 individual management team members and 90,000 investment rounds. Using this data, we examine how the co-investing relationships among VC firms affect the funding of WLBs. We proposed that those VC firms without strong social capital, created through co-investing with other VC firms, would be more likely to invest in WLBs. Our results were mixed. VC firms that co-invest with other VC firms that do not co-invest with one another invest in a lower percentage of investments in WLBs. This social capital measure is called "structural holes." VC firms with lower rates of structural holes invest in a higher percentage of WLBs. Another finding is that VC firms that have long-term co-investing relationships with other VC firms that co-invest frequently with these other firms invest in a higher percentage of WLBs when compared to VC firms without long-term relationships. Finally, our study finds that the performance of VC firms improves as the ratio of investment in WLBs increases. This study provides insights for VC firms looking to improve their performance and to WLBs searching for VC funding.

Chapter 3 – Since the 1990s, minority-oriented equity-capital funds, popularly known as venture capital (VC) funds, have substantially increased the size and scope of their small-business equity investments, particularly in firms owned by African Americans and Hispanics. Flush with capital raised from institutional investors in the 1990s, these venture-capital funds collectively have invested increasingly in new-economy high-tech lines of business in recent years. As high-tech investing has grown in popularity, the minority-oriented funds' investment practices have begun to resemble those of their mainstream (not minority oriented) VC-industry counterparts. This changing emphasis, along with a growing propensity to invest in white-owned firms, has coincided with substantial declines in the average returns generated by the minority-oriented VC funds in recent years. Why would these funds in the 21st century increasingly invest outside of their traditional minority-market niche? What are the ramifications of these investment trends for black- and Hispanic-owned ventures seeking venture capital financing? Why, finally, have the realized returns earned by the minority-oriented VC funds declined in the 21st century? Answers to these and closely related questions are developed and explained in this report.

Past studies have consistently demonstrated that minority-owned business enterprises (MBEs), particularly those owned by African Americans and Hispanics, have less access to debt and equity capital than similarly situated white-owned firms. When MBEs experience restricted access to capital markets, this market segment is being underserved and attractive returns may be available to funds choosing to specialize in financing this minority-business client group. This situation, which we call the "underserved market" hypothesis, indeed, constitutes the traditional rationale for the existence of minority-oriented VC funds.

We proceed by investigating the financial returns minority-oriented VC funds have earned on their realized equity investments initiated during the

1989 through 2004 time period. In cooperation with the National Association of Investment Companies (NAIC) and the E.M. Kauffman Foundation, extensive data describing the characteristics and strategies of VC funds serving the MBE market segment, along with detailed information on the equity investments in small businesses these funds have initiated since 1989, are now available to researchers. These data have been analyzed in this study. Our analysis sought to explain the financial returns generated by the investments of minority-oriented VC funds, and this was accomplished by analyzing detailed annual cash flow information through year end 2006 for each individual investment.

To understand the investment choices made by minority VC funds, it is necessary to situate those choices in the context of the strategies these funds employ to manage successfully the considerable risks inherent in making equity investments in their portfolio firms. Widespread syndication is symptomatic of the extensive networking that typifies the minority-oriented venture-capital funds. Through membership in the NAIC and their frequent cooperation in developing syndicated business investments, these funds are able to finance large deals while enhancing diversification of their investment portfolios. Second, nearly all of the VC fund general partners (GPs) actively participate in the affairs of their portfolio companies – sitting on boards of directors and involving the GPs in such managerial functions as assistance with hiring, engaging in active day-by-day managerial decision making, and participating in long-run planning. Finally, the minority-oriented VC funds, instead of focusing narrowly on a single industry, often rely on a diverse industry mix of portfolio companies; they are typically more broadly diversified than the mainstream venture-capital industry.

We have identified, using generalized least squares random effects regression analysis techniques, the fund traits and strategies that predict high investment returns on the realized equity investments of the minority-focused VC funds. We conducted these tests to determine the fund characteristics and strategies that are correlated with internal rates of return (IRR) values of individual VC investments in firms. Our analysis introduced control variables expected to impact investment returns, including equity investment dollar amounts, investment timing, portfolio company industry of operation, and VC fund vintage.

What profiles and strategies typify the more successful, as opposed to the less successful minority VC funds? Higher IRR values are associated with 1) investing in MBEs, 2) activism in assisting portfolio companies on the part of the VC fund general partners, and 3) a larger number of VC investments per fund general partner. It is noteworthy that all of these traits linked to higher returns on VC investments represent investing strategies employed at the discretion of the individual VC funds. Lower IRR values are associated with 1) making investments in white-owned firms, 2) being an older VC fund, 3) participating in syndicated investments, and 4) topof-the-cycle investing (making investments initially funded in either 1999 or 2000). Investing in high-tech companies, finally, has not been a productive strategy for minority-oriented VC funds seeking to generate high financial returns on their equity investments.

These findings validate the underserved minority market hypothesis: investing in MBEs, other factors being the same, generates higher returns for the minority VC funds than investments in nonminority-owned ventures. In English, this means that investments of the same dollar amount, initiated in the same time period, by minority-oriented VC funds using identical strategies regarding such factors as syndication, investment by industry, GP activism with portfolio companies, and the like, produced higher IRR values if the portfolio company was minority owned and lower values if the company was white owned.

Utilizing our regression analysis results and related findings, we attribute the generally declining financial returns typifying the minority-oriented VC funds in recent years to five factors, three of which reflect the tendency of these funds to emulate mainstream VC industry investing practices. First, cooperation among funds in the form of syndicated investing has declined, a trend mirroring mainstream investing practices. We attribute declining returns to the fact that minority VC funds are increasingly keeping their most promising investments entirely for themselves, while syndicating the less promising deals in order to spread the risk of a poor ultimate outcome for these deals. Second, the increasing frequency of investments in white-owned portfolio companies—rather than MBEs – has clearly depressed realized investment returns. Major institutional investors tend to prefer to provide investment capital to minority-oriented VC funds that emulate mainstream VC industry investing practices. Our analysis suggests that public pension funds and funds of funds – the two dominant sources of institutional investor funding for minority VC funds—collectively prefer to provide investment capital to minority VC funds investing in portfolio firms having racially diverse owners – white-owned as well as minority-owned ventures. Investing in hi-tech companies, third, is another factor tending to lower returns on realized equity investments in portfolio companies.

Investments initially funded in the years 1999 or 2000 by minority-oriented funds — investing at the very top of the VC industry's boom/bust cycle – were the fourth cause of low realized returns on VC investments; in comparison, investments initiated before or after 1999 and 2000 were much more successful. Investing heavily at the top of a boom/bust cycle, while certainly a negative, is most likely a transitory phenomenon rather than a strategic choice likely to indicate enduring poor returns on the equity investments made by the minority-oriented VC funds. Fund vintage, finally, shaped investing returns, a finding that suggests, on balance, a brighter future for the minority-oriented VC fund sector. The older funds were the ones most often producing low returns on realized equity investments, holding other factors constant, while the newer-generation funds – those most directly shaping the future trajectory – were the better performers. These newer VC funds are typically run by GPs possessing work experience in investment banking prior to launching their venture capital funds, while GPs of older funds rarely possessed such mainstream work experience. Our findings suggest that having prior work experience in investment banking conveyed investing advantages.

The question "why would these VC funds in the 21st century increasingly invest outside of their traditional minority market niche?" is closely linked to the investing preferences of the institutional investors that provide the funding for the venture capital industry. Major institutional investors like pension funds seek high financial returns when they invest in VC funds. When they contemplate investing into minority-oriented VC funds, they seek to cherry-pick the winners, investing only in the subset of minority funds poised to generate above-average returns for their institutional investors. In the process of picking and choosing those funds potentially offering the highest investment returns, the institutional investors effectively shape the trajectory of the minority VC industry subsector. The winners—flush with funding —rapidly achieve growing prominence in the MBE equity investing realm; the losers—smaller in resources available for investing—lose relative position within the minority VC fund universe.

Our findings and those of other researchers indicate that the dominant institutional investors providing funding to the minority-oriented VC funds have systematically tended to invest in the less profitable VC funds, including those investing most actively in hi-tech and white-owned portfolio companies. Importantly, however, the investing practices of these institutional capital sources are self-correcting over time precisely because their funding decisions are driven largely by their search for above-average returns. We therefore see this institutional investor set of preferences as a short-term phenomenon, with future funding flowing increasingly to the minority-oriented VC funds pursuing the equity investing strategies most clearly identified with generating high returns on their VC investments. Investing in minority-owned business ventures will remain dominant because they offer higher returns, on balance, than investments in firms owned by nonminority whites.

In: Capital Access   ISBN: 978-1-62948-197-5
Editors: H. Drexler and G. Maines   © 2013 Nova Science Publishers, Inc.

Chapter 1

ACCESS TO CAPITAL AMONG YOUNG FIRMS, MINORITY-OWNED FIRMS, WOMEN-OWNED FIRMS, AND HIGH-TECH FIRMS[*]

Alicia Robb

EXECUTIVE SUMMARY

This report examines access to capital by young and small businesses. The purpose of the investigation is to gain a better understanding of access to capital by young firms and how the recent economic and financial crisis has affected their access to financial capital, especially among firms owned by women and minorities and firms that are high tech in nature. In light of the key role in small business finance played by financial institutions, this study pays disproportionate attention to access to bank loans. Although these issues are important, research has traditionally been limited by a lack of appropriate data. A primary obstacle has been the absence of representative samples of small businesses that contain detailed descriptions of their access to financing. The primary source of data on this question, the Federal Reserve Survey of Small Business Finances, was discontinued in 2003, and is thus unavailable for studying the effects of the financial crisis on small businesses.

---

[*] This report, released April 2013, was written by Alicia Robb of Marin Consulting, LLC under a contract with the Small Business Administration, Office of Advocacy

A second obstacle has been the tendency of researchers to analyze data on cross sections of small businesses of varying ages and sizes at a single point in time. While the findings from these snapshots have been valuable to scholars and policymakers, they have also been limited. Because they are static, these snapshots do not capture the ways in which small business financing unfolds over the life cycle of the firm and changes over time. This study attempts to overcome these obstacles by examining the effects of the changing financial environment generally and the economic crisis specifically, on access to capital by small businesses over the 2004 through 2010 period, controlling for business and owner characteristics. Analyses of small-firm capital access are based upon firm subsets drawn from the Kauffman Firm Survey.

Key findings of this study include the fact that firms owned by African Americans and Latinos utilize a different mix of equity and debt capital, relative to firms owned by nonminorities. Relying disproportionately upon owner equity investments and employing relatively less debt from outside sources (primarily banks), the average firm in these minority business subgroups operates with substantially less capital overall – both at startup and in subsequent years – relative to their nonminority counterparts. Women-owned businesses exhibit some similar disparities in capital structure, relative to male-owned firms, in the sense of operating with much less capital, on average, and a somewhat different mix of debt and equity capital. Their reliance upon outside equity capital is particularly low. The initial disparities in the levels of startup capital by business owner race, ethnicity, and gender do not disappear in the subsequent years following startup.

The information asymmetry inherent with new and young firms is exacerbated in high technology industries due to the lack of tangible assets and their reliance on knowledge assets, as well as technical and market uncertainty. The information asymmetries associated with new firms in general, and high tech firms specifically, make traditional bank lenders less likely to lend to these firms. This report also examines financing patters of high tech firms.

This study will help government officials document significant racial and gender disparities in capital access, differences in lending patterns between high tech and non-high tech firms, and credit market conditions during the financial crisis. These results will help policymakers in developing policies to ensure optimal access to debt and equity capital among all small businesses, including during times of financial stress.

BACKGROUND

Access to capital for small businesses is one of the biggest policy issues in the United States today. This work has important implications for policy and policymakers at all levels. In particular, given the role of young firms and entrepreneurs in job creation and economic growth, policymakers need to ensure that entrepreneurs and creditworthy firms are able to secure adequate financial resources for growth and success. Ensuring that these firms have adequate access to financial capital enables them to continue to drive innovation, growth, and job creation in the U.S. economy.

The economics and finance literatures provide strong evidence that sufficient starting capital is a binding constraint for new firms. Entry into entrepreneurship increases with sudden increases in personal wealth, e.g. via bequest (Cagetti and De Nardi (2006)) or external change in taxation rate (Nanda (2008)), and with increased access to bank financing through deregulation and loosening of branching restrictions (Black and Strahan (2002)). Likewise, the absence of funds inhibits entry. For example, Evans and Jovanovic (1989) find that borrowing capacity limits entrepreneurial entry; using the National Longitudinal Survey they estimate that new entrepreneurs are limited by the size of their initial assets in starting a new business. So inequalities in personal wealth could translate into disparities in business creation and ownership.

We certainly see disparities in business ownership by race, ethnicity, and gender. The most recent statistics available from the Census Bureau come from the 2007 Survey of Business Owners (SBO). These data showed that women-owned firms made up 28.7 percent of the 27.1 million businesses in the United States, while minorities owned 21.3 percent of businesses. Clearly women and minorities are underrepresented in business ownership in this country, compared with white men. As the minority population continues to rise, it is more important than ever that these prospective business owners have the resources they need to launch successful firms. Financial capital is one such resource and previous research shows that much of the financial capital used to start businesses comes from the owners themselves.

Yet estimates from the U.S. Census Bureau indicate that half of all Hispanic families have less than $13,375 in wealth, and half of all African-American families less than $8,650 (Table1). Wealth levels among non-minorities are much higher. African-American wealth levels are just 8 percent of non-minority wealth levels, and Hispanic wealth levels are just 12 percent of non-minority wealth levels. Only Asians have wealth levels similar to those of non-Hispanic Whites. Low levels of wealth and liquidity constraints can create substantial barriers to entry for would-be entrepreneurs because the owner's wealth can be invested directly in the business, used as collateral to obtain business loans, or used to acquire other businesses. Investors frequently require a substantial level of an owner's investment of his/her own capital as an incentive.

Table 1. Median Household Net Worth by Ethnicity/Race, 2004

	Median Net Worth	As a % of Non-minority
Total	$ 79,800	
Non-minority	$ 113,822	100%
Asian or Pac. Islander	$ 107,690	94.6%
Hispanic	$ 13,375	11.8%
African-American	$ 8,650	7.6%

Source: U.S. Census Bureau, Housing and Household Economic Statistics Division (2011).

Previous studies find that relatively low levels of wealth among Hispanics and African Americans contribute to these groups having lower business creation rates relative to their representation in the U.S. population. Fairlie (2006) found that differences in asset levels are the largest single factor explaining racial disparities in business creation rates. He found that lower levels of assets among African Americans account for more than 15 percent of the difference between the rates of business creation among Whites and Blacks. Fairlie (2006) also found that differences in asset levels represented a major hindrance for business creation among Hispanics, while Fairlie and Woodruff (2009) studied the causes of low rates of business formation among Mexican-Americans in particular. An important factor that explains one-quarter of the business entry rate gap between Mexican-Americans and non-Hispanic Whites is asset levels.

Less research has focused on the related question of whether low levels of personal wealth and liquidity constraints also limit the ability of minority entrepreneurs to raise adequate levels of startup capital. Fairlie and Robb (2008) found that undercapitalized businesses had lower sales, profits, and employment, and were more likely to fail than businesses receiving optimal levels of startup capital. The common use of personal commitments to obtain business loans suggests that wealthier entrepreneurs may be able to negotiate better credit terms and obtain larger loans for their new businesses, possibly leading to more successful firms (Astebro and Berhardt (2003)). Cavalluzzo and Wolken (2005) also found that personal wealth, primarily through home ownership, decreases the probability of loan denials among existing business owners. If personal wealth is important for existing business owners in acquiring business loans then it may be even more important for entrepreneurs in acquiring startup loans.

Previous research indicates that the level of startup capital is a strong predictor of business success. (Bates (1997); Fairlie and Robb (2008)). Asian firms are found to have higher startup capital levels and resulting business outcomes (Fairlie and Robb (2008). As noted, their wealth levels are also on par with Whites. Therefore, I will focus on Blacks, Hispanics, and other non-Asians as one group, and compare them with Whites. I will also look at men and women separately.

Much of the recent research on the issue of discrimination in business lending uses data from various years of the Survey of Small Business Finances (SSBF). The main finding from this literature is that MBEs experience higher loan denial probabilities and pay higher interest rates than White-owned businesses even after controlling for differences in creditworthiness, and other factors.[1] Cavalluzzo and Wolken (2005) found that while greater personal wealth is associated with a lower probability of denial, even after controlling for personal wealth, there remained a large difference in denial rates across demographic groups. African Americans, Hispanics, and Asians were all more likely to be denied credit, compared with Whites, even after controlling for a number of owner and firm characteristics, including credit history, credit score, and wealth. They also found that Hispanics and African Americans were more likely to pay higher interest rates on the loans they obtained. Using the 2003 SSBF, Blanchflower (2007) also found Asian-Americans, Hispanics and African Americans were more likely than Whites to be denied credit, even after controlling for creditworthiness and other factors.

Banks have historically provided new firms with crucial growth capital, and have played a substantial role in new firm formation and business expansion both in the United States and internationally (Ayyagari, Demirguc-Kunt and Maksimovic (2010); Beck, Demirgüç-Kunt and Maksimovic (2008); Kerr and Nanda (2009)); Robb and Robinson (2012)). Black and Strahan (2002) show that deregulation of interstate banking and loosening of branching restrictions fostered increased entrepreneurial activity.

In times of financial distress, however, bank lending may be curtailed, with decreased lending potentially reflecting a "flight to quality" (Caballero and Krishnamurthy, 2008). Such effects have been pronounced in the wake of events such as the failure of Lehman Brothers in 2008 (Ivashina and Scharfstein, 2010), and more generally, in response to recessions (Gertler and Gilchrist, 1994; Holmstrom and Tirole, 1997)). Moreover, the flight to quality is seen as having a greater effect on firms more subject to agency problems and information opacity (Gertler and Gilchrist, 1994).

If banks do indeed avoid making riskier loans in times of financial crisis, then it stands to reason that firms that are *inherently* more risky—such as young firms and firms in industries characterized by greater technical or market uncertainty—might be most affected by such events. One important question that the literature has not addressed is how the lending response in a financial crisis affects the youngest firms in general, and in particular, whether there might be a disproportionate impact on the riskiest of these firms (e.g., those in high technology industries). I will investigate the financing constraints of high tech firms specifically, in addition to firms owned by women and minorities.

In previous work using the KFS data, Winston Smith (2011) provided evidence that banks increase lending to high technology firms as information asymmetry and inherent uncertainty surrounding the firm are lessened. While high tech firms account for a relatively small percent of the full population of firms, they are disproportionately likely to contribute to economic growth through employment, revenue, assets, and innovations. Hence, access to sufficient financial capital for these firms is paramount to our economic recovery.

Data and Univariate Statistics

In this study, I examine the financing patterns of young firms during their early years of existence. The data are from the Kauffman Firm Survey, a nationally representative cohort of businesses that began operations in 2004, which are followed over the 2004 to 2010 period. One item of note is that these data represent a cohort of firms that began in 2004; the data are not representative of all startups or all businesses in the United States. New businesses were defined as having done one or more of the following activities in 2004 and not prior: (1) state unemployment insurance (UI) payments; (2) Federal Insurance Contributions Act (FICA) tax payments made for the first time in the targeted year for the classification of a new business; (3) filing for legal business status (sole proprietorship, general partnership, limited partnership, C corporation, subchapter S corporation, and limited liability company); (4) acquisition of an Employer Identification Number (EIN); and/or (5) use of an Internal Revenue Service Schedule C or C-EZ as part of the owner's income tax return. The sampling frame for the KFS was the Dun & Bradstreet (D&B) database and restricted to businesses (or enterprises) reported by D&B as having started in 2004. This database is a compilation of data from various sources, including credit bureaus and state offices that register new firms, as well as companies (e.g., credit card and shipping companies) that are likely to be used by all businesses.

The survey questionnaire covered a variety of topics, including business characteristics, strategy and innovation, business structure and benefits, financing, and demographics of the business owners. The KFS currently contains data on the baseline (calendar year 2004) and six follow up years (2005-2010). The method used for assigning owner demographics at the firm level was to define a primary owner. For firms with multiple owners (35 percent of the sample), the primary owner was designated by the largest equity share. In cases in which two or more owners had equal shares, hours worked and a series of other variables were used to create a rank ordering in order to define a primary owner. (For more information on this methodology, see Robb et al. 2009).

A public-use dataset is available for download from the Kauffman Foundation's web site and a more detailed confidential dataset is available to researchers through a secure, remote access data enclave provided by the National Opinion Research Center (NORC). For more details about how to access these data, please see www.kauffman.org/kfs. This report uses the confidential microdata.

While 2004, the year in which the KFS firms started, was pretty average in most respects, the KFS firms faced an economic crisis in their early years of operation that was anything but average. This crisis began affecting firms in 2008, but the impact of the crisis continued over the period 2008-2010. When asked to report if they applied and obtained loans or lines of credit and the reasons why these applications were not filed or were denied, access to credit seemed to be an issue for many firms. Unfortunately, the Kauffman Firm Survey only began asking questions about new loan applications, fear of denial, and loan application outcomes beginning in 2007. So there is only one year of data on these questions in the pre-crisis period. Because of this, I focus on the years 2007-2010 in the subsequent analysis. Thus, the firms analyzed are KFS businesses that began operations in 2004 and survived through 2007. I do show all seven years of data for financing patterns that are available.

As shown in Table 2, the 2007 means of various firm and owner characteristics of the sample are presented. The first column contains those owned by Whites, while the second column contains firms owned by owners that are Black/Hispanic/Other, not including Asians. The next two columns are female-owned and male-owned firms, respectively. The final column contains firms that are considered to be high tech or technology based firms.

Female-owned firms were slightly less likely to have high credit scores, compared with men. Blacks and Hispanics were much less likely than Whites to own firms with high credit scores with only 7 percent of minority-owned firms having a high credit score, compared with nearly double that for Whites (13.7 percent). High tech firms were the group with the highest proportion of firms with high credit scores (15.9 percent). This influences capital access, which will be discussed in the next section.

Table 2. Firm and Owner Characteristics of Kauffman Firm Survey Businesses

Firm Characteristics	White	Black/ Hispanic	Female	Male	High Tech
High Credit Score	13.7%	7.2%	12.1%	13.6%	15.9%
Medium Credit Score	56.1%	52.8%	55.0%	55.2%	62.7%
Low Credit Score	30.1%	39.5%	32.6%	31.1%	21.1%
Incorporated	57.1%	51.1%	47.1%	60.9%	71.5%
Intellectual Property	19.9%	19.8%	18.7%	20.6%	37.5%
Product Offerings	51.2%	52.1%	50.7%	51.1%	52.0%
Team Ownership	31.6%	26.8%	29.4%	32.1%	37.1%
Home Based	50.9%	51.6%	51.7%	49.5%	51.6%
Owner Characteristics					
Net Wealth of $250K+ (2008)	45.4%	20.6%	41.1%	42.2%	52.4%
Ave Hours Worked (week)	42.7	43.5	40.1	44.3	44.3
Prev.Years of Industry Experience	12.8	11.6	9.5	13.7	16.1
Owner Age	45.8	42.8	45.1	45.3	44.9
Some College	36.3%	43.2%	40.8%	34.6%	22.6%
College Degree	32.7%	27.7%	29.4%	33.5%	34.5%
Graduate Degree+	18.2%	15.7%	19.7%	18.3%	36.9%

Firm Characteristics	White	Black/ Hispanic	Female	Male	High Tech
Previous Startup Experience	44.3%	38.1%	37.0%	45.8%	46.1%
Industry					
Manufacturing	5.6%	9.0%	6.1%	6.2%	10.4%
Wholesale	4.9%	6.3%	5.5%	5.0%	0.0%
Retail	14.0%	12.9%	16.8%	12.4%	0.0%
Transportation and Warehousing	2.6%	4.9%	2.3%	3.0%	0.0%
Finance, Insurance, Real Estate	14.0%	14.6%	12.5%	14.8%	13.4%
Professional Services	19.4%	17.9%	16.9%	20.2%	76.2%
Admin and Support, Health Care	12.7%	13.4%	16.8%	11.6%	0.0%
Arts, Entertain., & Recreation	4.8%	1.4%	4.5%	4.4%	0.0%
Other Services	11.2%	8.0%	13.4%	9.4%	0.0%
Sample size (surviving until at least 2007)	2,086	326	637	1,900	357

There are quite a few differences across the race and gender groups in terms of firm and owner characteristics. Most notably, women-owned firms are less likely to be incorporated, compared with firms owned by men. Minorities follow a similar pattern, much lower, compared with Whites. High tech firms are the most likely to be incorporated, to have intellectual property, and to have team ownership.

Women owners tend to have fewer years of industry experience, as well as startup experience, compared with men. Blacks and Hispanics have slightly lower average industry experience and education, and much less startup experience, compared with Whites. In addition, only about 20 percent of minorities have wealth levels of $250,000 or more, compared with more than 45 percent of Whites. Again, high tech firms had the highest shares of high net worth individuals, the highest education levels, and the highest levels of industry and startup experience.

Credit market experience also differs across racial and gender groups (Table 3). Women, Blacks, and Hispanics were less likely to apply for new loans than their male and White counterparts. High tech firms had the highest rate of new loan applications in 2007 (17 percent). Women were slightly more likely than men to say that they didn't apply for credit when they needed it at some point during the year because they feared their loan application would be denied. Black- and Hispanic owners were nearly three times as likely to have this fear, compared with White owners. Nearly one third of Black- and Hispanic owners stated they had this fear in 2007, and the percentage was even higher in the years of the financial crisis.

In terms of the outcomes of loan applications, we also see different patterns. Black- and Hispanic owned firms were much less likely to have their loans approved. Females had lower approval rates than men, except for 2007. We see the approval rates drop in the years of the financial crisis. High tech firms had initially much lower rates of approval for loan applications, but had higher than average rates of approval in subsequent years.

Table 3. Credit Market Experiences (2007-2010)

2007	All	White	Black/Hispanic	Female	Male	High Tech
New Loan Application	12.3%	12.9%	9.4%	9.9%	13.0%	17.0%
Did not Apply for Fear	15.7%	13.2%	31.3%	16.9%	15.3%	15.2%
Always Approved	70.9%	75.8%	31.5%	74.2%	70.1%	49.6%
2008	All	White	Black/Hispanic	Female	Male	High Tech
New Loan Application	11.2%	11.0%	7.7%	8.1%	12.0%	11.1%
Did not Apply for Fear	18.9%	14.7%	39.3%	21.4%	17.0%	20.7%
Always Approved	61.9%	68.9%	29.7%	60.4%	65.2%	70.5%
2009	All	White	Black/Hispanic	Female	Male	High Tech
New Loan Application	12.3%	12.1%	12.3%	10.6%	12.7%	16.4%
Did not Apply for Fear	21.4%	18.1%	40.0%	23.9%	20.2%	18.9%
Always Approved	60.6%	64.7%	32.7%	52.8%	62.9%	63.8%
2010	All	White	Black/Hispanic	Female	Male	High Tech
New Loan Application	11.1%	11.0%	7.3%	8.0%	12.0%	10.5%
Did not Apply for Fear	19.2%	15.2%	38.8%	21.1%	17.8%	21.1%
Always Approved	60.7%	67.4%	28.2%	59.5%	63.2%	71.1%

Source: KFS Microdata.

Of course, these are univariate statistics and they do not control for differences in business quality, industry, managerial quality, etc. We will investigate this more fully in a multivariate framework. But first, let's take a look at the financing patterns of these businesses at startup and over time.

I follow the classification scheme from Robb and Robinson (2012) that distinguishes funding sources in terms of both their security type (debt vs. equity) and their source (personal accounts of the business owner(s) vs. friends and family vs. arm's length formal financial channels). This two-way classification scheme allows one to separate the issue of risk-bearing from that of liquidity provision. For example, if an entrepreneur uses a home equity line of credit from a bank to finance a startup, the entrepreneur is bearing the risk of failure through a levered equity stake in the business, but the bank is providing liquidity to the business through a debt instrument to the entrepreneur. Because many startups are sole proprietorships, and many that are not are financed with personal guarantees and personal wealth as collateral, distinguishing risk-bearing from liquidity provision is important for understanding how startups are financed. The distinction between risk-bearing and liquidity provision is a direct consequence of the bank's ability to contractually sidestep limited liability through the use of the owner's personal assets as a guarantee.

Most theoretical treatments of capital structure explicitly or implicitly assume that limited liability implies that a borrower cannot claim more than the value of the business in question. However, empirical research on small business lending has shown that personal guarantees and personal collateral must often be posted to secure financing for startups (Moon 2009; Avery, Bostic, and Samalyk 1998; Mann 1998). This means that limited liability constraints can be contractually circumvented in the borrower/lender agreement with a bank by requiring the borrower to pledge personal assets that may exceed the value of the business if it fails. The fact that limited liability constraints can be circumvented in small business lending relationships implies that there is a critical distinction between liquidity provision and risk bearing in financing relationships.

The logic above suggests that a natural way to classify financing decisions is first to distinguish between type of security (i.e., equity vs. debt) and then also to distinguish capital according to its source (i.e., formal vs. informal). The justification for this stems from the fact that different providers of capital may have access to different enforcement technologies. For example, informal lenders, such as friends and family, may have little ability to seize collateral, and therefore the expected return to debt for them is low; this may lead them to prefer equity over debt.

Capital can be provided either by owners, insiders, or outsiders. The KFS is careful to distinguish owner equity from cash that a business owner obtained through, say, a home equity line, which in this classification scheme would be a source of outside debt, since it was provided through a formal contract with a lending institution. Informal financing channels include debt or equity from family members and personal affiliates of the firm, whereas formal financing channels include debt accessed through formal credit markets (banks, credit cards, and lines of credit) as well as venture capital and angel financing.

Thus, I group together personal debt on the business owner's household balance sheet with business bank loans, and I place these under the □outside debt" category. For much of the sample the distinction between personal and business debt is meaningless because the business is structured as a sole proprietorship. For the businesses organized as corporations and partnerships, no information is available about which firms relied on personal guarantees and the use of personal assets as collateral, but the work of Moon (2009), Avery, Bostic, and Samalyk (1998), Mann (1998), and others suggests that these channels are important. The primary distinction is not whether the debt is a claim on the business owner's household or business assets, but rather whether the debt was issued by an institution or by friends and family.

Table 4 describes the levels of financial capital invested in the startup year and for each year of observation. Just to be clear, in the years 2007-2010, these are new financial injections at each year in time. The levels of startup capital differ significantly across the groups. Blacks and Hispanics start their firms with about half the capital that Whites use. Women follow a similar pattern, starting their firms with a little over half of what men invest. These are large differences that persist over time; in fact, the disparities actually widened in some subsequent years.

High tech firms started with the highest levels of financial capital and were the most reliant on outsider equity (venture capital, angel investment, etc.). This pattern continued in the later years as well. These firms invested the most financial capital and were the most reliant on outsider equity. They were less reliant on outsider debt, compared with firms on average, which is some evidence for banks preferring to fund less informationally opaque borrowers, especially during times of financial stress. This is consistent with findings from Robb and Seamans (2012) and Robb and Winston-Smith (2012).

Table 4. Financial Capital Investments (2004, 2007-2010)

2004	All	White	Black/ Hispanic	Female	Male	High Tech
Owner Equity	$ 33,061	$ 33,099	$ 24,777	$ 24,556	$ 36,807	$ 29,667
Insider Equity	$ 2,055	$ 1,881	$ 1,049	$ 2,043	$ 1,880	$ 2,983
Outsider Equity	$ 15,509	$ 17,292	$ 1,070	$ 1,272	$ 22,293	$ 46,749
Owner Debt	$ 4,618	$ 5,131	$ 2,521	$ 3,650	$ 5,101	$ 6,367
Insider Debt	$ 6,437	$ 6,265	$ 4,362	$ 5,577	$ 6,975	$ 3,524
Outsider Debt	$ 50,031	$ 53,809	$ 24,907	$ 36,400	$ 57,110	$ 28,133
Total Financial Capital	$ 111,712	$ 117,477	$ 58,687	$ 73,500	$ 130,166	$ 117,424
2007						
Owner Equity	$ 10,280	$ 9,874	$ 6,758	$ 8,699	$ 10,801	$ 28,075
Insider Equity	$ 580	$ 532	$ 1,107	$ 271	$ 733	$ 2,688
Outsider Equity	$ 8,531	$ 9,814	$ 4,260	$ 2,205	$ 11,534	$ 23,575
Owner Debt	$ 4,219	$ 4,697	$ 2,314	$ 5,929	$ 3,602	$ 6,228
Insider Debt	$ 4,967	$ 6,014	$ 1,715	$ 1,294	$ 6,708	$ 3,500
Outsider Debt	$ 53,315	$ 57,411	$ 17,404	$ 34,695	$ 56,974	$ 36,226
Total Financial Capital	$ 81,892	$ 88,342	$ 33,557	$ 53,092	$ 90,352	$ 100,292
2008						
Owner Equity	$ 10,749	$ 9,683	$ 5,802	$ 6,499	$ 11,026	$ 29,307
Insider Equity	$ 549	$ 431	$ 1,519	$ 324	$ 668	$ 3,298
Outsider Equity	$ 5,591	$ 5,515	$ 5,874	$ 1,113	$ 7,592	$ 44,423
Owner Debt	$ 4,411	$ 4,180	$ 6,289	$ 4,255	$ 4,608	$ 6,934
Insider Debt	$ 3,354	$ 3,119	$ 2,851	$ 2,995	$ 3,123	$ 8,166
Outsider Debt	$ 47,525	$ 44,642	$ 19,329	$ 32,105	$ 46,742	$ 40,341
Total Financial Capital	$ 72,180	$ 67,571	$ 41,664	$ 47,291	$ 73,758	$ 132,471
2009						
Owner Equity	$ 8,416	$ 7,893	$ 6,102	$ 3,244	$ 9,908	$ 17,926
Insider Equity	$ 799	$ 358	$ 73	$ 113	$ 1,063	$ 93
Outsider Equity	$ 5,448	$ 5,681	$ 626	$ 1,690	$ 7,270	$ 37,244
Owner Debt	$ 2,850	$ 3,083	$ 1,916	$ 3,320	$ 2,705	$ 3,076
Insider Debt	$ 5,891	$ 5,447	$ 4,692	$ 2,706	$ 7,289	$ 10,466
Outsider Debt	$ 50,029	$ 50,000	$ 19,806	$ 14,992	$ 64,729	$ 49,293
Total Financial Capital	$ 73,432	$ 72,463	$ 33,214	$ 26,064	$ 92,964	$ 118,099
2010						
Owner Equity	$ 6,586	$ 6,214	$ 4,145	$ 4,855	$ 6,668	$ 5,616
Insider Equity	$ 1,467	$ 1,457	$ 155	$ 62	$ 1,696	$ 458
Outsider Equity	$ 10,338	$ 7,701	$ 2,265	$ 1,131	$ 9,382	$ 14,569

Table 4. (Continued)

2004	All	White	Black/Hispanic	Female	Male	High Tech
Owner Debt	$ 2,942	$ 3,068	$ 2,084	$ 3,072	$ 2,916	$ 1,380
Insider Debt	$ 5,893	$ 5,968	$ 2,878	$ 5,198	$ 6,085	$ 7,193
Outsider Debt	$ 45,633	$ 43,525	$ 20,153	$ 23,899	$ 46,503	$ 32,104
Total Financial Capital	$ 72,859	$ 67,934	$ 31,681	$ 38,217	$ 73,249	$ 61,321

In terms of the relative importance of the various sources of financing, we also see large differences by race and gender here. As shown in Table 5, Blacks and Hispanics were relatively more reliant than Whites on owner financing, and the same held true for subsequent financial injections. For women, however, the large disparity seems to be driven primarily by the lack of external equity, although women were slightly more reliant on owner financing than were men. High tech firms were most reliant on outsider equity and less reliant on the other sources, both at startup and in subsequent years.

Table 5. Distribution of Financial Capital Investments (2004, 2007-2010)

2004	All	White	Black/Hispanic	Female	Male	High Tech
Owner Equity	29.6%	28.2%	42.2%	33.4%	28.3%	25.3%
Insider Equity	1.8%	1.6%	1.8%	2.8%	1.4%	2.5%
Outsider Equity	13.9%	14.7%	1.8%	1.7%	17.1%	39.8%
Owner Debt	4.1%	4.4%	4.3%	5.0%	3.9%	5.4%
Insider Debt	5.8%	5.3%	7.4%	7.6%	5.4%	3.0%
Outsider Debt	44.8%	45.8%	42.4%	49.5%	43.9%	24.0%
Total Financial Capital	100.0%	100.0%	100.0%	100.0%	100.0%	100.0%
2007						
Owner Equity	12.6%	11.2%	20.1%	16.4%	12.0%	28.0%
Insider Equity	0.7%	0.6%	3.3%	0.5%	0.8%	2.7%
Outsider Equity	10.4%	11.1%	12.7%	4.2%	12.8%	23.5%
Owner Debt	5.2%	5.3%	6.9%	11.2%	4.0%	6.2%
Insider Debt	6.1%	6.8%	5.1%	2.4%	7.4%	3.5%
Outsider Debt	65.1%	65.0%	51.9%	65.3%	63.1%	36.1%
Total Financial Capital	100.0%	100.0%	100.0%	100.0%	100.0%	100.0%

2008						
Owner Equity	14.9%	14.3%	13.9%	13.7%	14.9%	22.1%
Insider Equity	0.8%	0.6%	3.6%	0.7%	0.9%	2.5%
Outsider Equity	7.7%	8.2%	14.1%	2.4%	10.3%	33.5%
Owner Debt	6.1%	6.2%	15.1%	9.0%	6.2%	5.2%
Insider Debt	4.6%	4.6%	6.8%	6.3%	4.2%	6.2%
Outsider Debt	65.8%	66.1%	46.4%	67.9%	63.4%	30.5%
Total Financial Capital	100.0%	100.0%	100.0%	100.0%	100.0%	100.0%
2009						
Owner Equity	11.5%	10.9%	18.4%	12.4%	10.7%	15.2%
Insider Equity	1.1%	0.5%	0.2%	0.4%	1.1%	0.1%
Outsider Equity	7.4%	7.8%	1.9%	6.5%	7.8%	31.5%
Owner Debt	3.9%	4.3%	5.8%	12.7%	2.9%	2.6%
Insider Debt	8.0%	7.5%	14.1%	10.4%	7.8%	8.9%
Outsider Debt	68.1%	69.0%	59.6%	57.5%	69.6%	41.7%
Total Financial Capital	100.0%	100.0%	100.0%	100.0%	100.0%	100.0%
2010						
Owner Equity	9.0%	9.1%	13.1%	12.7%	9.1%	9.2%
Insider Equity	2.0%	2.1%	0.5%	0.2%	2.3%	0.7%
Outsider Equity	14.2%	11.3%	7.2%	3.0%	12.8%	23.8%
Owner Debt	4.0%	4.5%	6.6%	8.0%	4.0%	2.3%
Insider Debt	8.1%	8.8%	9.1%	13.6%	8.3%	11.7%
Outsider Debt	62.6%	64.1%	63.6%	62.5%	63.5%	52.4%
Total Financial Capital	100.0%	100.0%	100.0%	100.0%	100.0%	100.0%

Multivariate Analysis

When looking at loan applications, application outcomes, fear of denial, and lending patterns, it is necessary to use a multivariate framework, as these actions are related to a number of factors. The models used here draw on standard assumptions in the banking literature (Gorton and Winton, 2003). The decision to apply for a bank loan in year t is modelled as a function of growth prospects and degree of credit/liquidity constraint as well as control variables for industry, firm size, and owner characteristics (Chava and Purnanandam, 2011; Edelstein, 1975). The role of information asymmetry in mediating the loan application and approval process is also examined by using two proxies for information asymmetry. Particularly for a new firm, having a credit rating inherently reduces the information asymmetry between loan applicant and lender (Gorton and Winton, 2003). I use the Dun & Bradstreet credit score to define those in the top 20 percent of the credit score distribution as being highly creditworthy and then the next set of about 50 percent of firms designated as having medium creditworthiness. These are included as predictors of applying for a loan as well as the loan application outcome. The credit score provides significant information to the lender about the creditworthiness of the applicant, thereby reducing the information asymmetry.

I also follow a previous study that looks at the role of intellectual property in bank lending decisions (Winston Smith, 2011) and use a dummy variable to reflect a firm's use of intellectual property in terms of patents, trademarks, and copyrights. Finally, I include controls for firm and owner characteristics that have been shown in the previous literature to affect the likelihood of bank borrowing. Firm characteristics include credit score, a dummy for high tech, legal form of ownership, offering a product (vs. a service), and team ownership. Owner characteristics include race, ethnicity, gender, and age. I also include measures of the owner's human capital, including education, years of prior industry experience, and prior startup experience. Industry is controlled for at the two-digit NAICS level, but not presented in the tables because of space constraints. Each year is run separately.

$$\text{Loan app} = \alpha + \beta(\text{firm characteristics}) + \Omega(\text{owner characteristics}) + \text{industry controls} + \varepsilon \tag{1}$$

$$\text{Fear} = \alpha + \beta(\text{firm characteristics}) + \Omega(\text{owner characteristics}) + \text{industry controls} + \varepsilon \tag{2}$$

$$\text{Approval} = \alpha + \beta(\text{firm characteristics}) + \Omega(\text{owner characteristics}) + \text{industry controls} + \varepsilon \tag{3}$$

Thus, to summarize, the empirical approach used in this report is to estimate separate maximum likelihood logistic regressions on the probability of applying for a loan, the probability of not applying for a loan when credit is needed for fear of having the loan application denied, and the probability of receiving a loan. Please see the appendix for variable definitions.

The first result that stands out is that the coefficient on the minority dummy (which includes Blacks, Hispanics, and business owners of other races (other than Asian)) is negative in all years and statistically significant in 2007 and 2008. This means that this group is less likely to apply for new loans, compared with their White counterparts. It appears that women were no more or less likely to apply for new loans than men, controlling for other factors. High tech firms were more likely to apply for loans than non-high tech firms in 2007-2009, but the difference was statistically significant only in 2007 and 2009.

In terms of important firm and owner characteristics, firms that were incorporated and firms with teams and owners with higher education levels were more likely to apply for new credit. Having intellectual property did not seem to play any role in loan applications. Being home based was associated with a lower likelihood of applying for a loan.

Table 6. New Loan Application(s)

VARIABLES	2007	2008	2009	2010
Black/ Hispanic	-0.419*	-0.763***	-0.102	-0.482
	(0.242)	(0.281)	(0.267)	(0.315)
Asian	-0.731	-0.470	-0.585	0.431
	(0.464)	(0.498)	(0.439)	(0.400)
Female	-0.141	-0.0114	0.0866	-0.245
	(0.205)	(0.220)	(0.208)	(0.240)
High Tech	0.482*	0.327	0.507*	-0.0570
	(0.248)	(0.277)	(0.278)	(0.319)
High Credit Score	0.222	0.454*	0.320	0.870***
	(0.261)	(0.262)	(0.275)	(0.310)
Medium Credit Score	0.154	0.155	-0.0151	0.356
	(0.195)	(0.204)	(0.218)	(0.244)
Incorporated	0.580***	0.533***	0.902***	0.721***
	(0.191)	(0.204)	(0.225)	(0.243)
Intellectual Property	0.0140	0.0605	0.172	0.318
	(0.197)	(0.200)	(0.198)	(0.226)
Product Offering(s)	0.265	0.243	-0.105	-0.0108
	(0.191)	(0.187)	(0.205)	(0.219)
Home Based	-0.395**	-0.317*	-0.553***	-0.474**
	(0.164)	(0.183)	(0.191)	(0.208)
Hours Worked	0.00895***	0.00517	0.00581	0.00120
	(0.00346)	(0.00355)	(0.00405)	(0.00405)
Industry Experience	0.00721	0.0142	-0.00925	0.0120
	(0.00882)	(0.00920)	(0.00915)	(0.00969)

Table 6. (Continued)

VARIABLES	2007	2008	2009	2010
Age	0.0129	-0.0695	-0.0524	0.0369
	(0.0499)	(0.0522)	(0.0535)	(0.0622)
Team Ownership	0.216	0.602***	0.387**	0.100
	(0.174)	(0.173)	(0.187)	(0.204)
Age Squared	-0.000333	0.000477	0.000664	-0.000612
	(0.000520)	(0.000544)	(0.000558)	(0.000656)
Some College	0.589*	0.637**	0.242	-0.249
	(0.323)	(0.316)	(0.357)	(0.339)
College Degree	0.822**	0.700**	0.575	-0.0412
	(0.323)	(0.328)	(0.365)	(0.352)
Graduate Degree+	0.793**	0.658*	0.720*	0.162
	(0.340)	(0.359)	(0.392)	(0.381)
Startup Experience	0.0964	0.154	-0.110	-0.100
	(0.164)	(0.167)	(0.178)	(0.199)
Constant	-2.969**	-1.370	-1.781	-2.882*
	(1.227)	(1.270)	(1.316)	(1.535)
Observations	2,724	2,434	2,168	1,959

Excluded dummies: White, High School Degree or Less, Low Credit Score Standard errors in parentheses.

*** p<0.01, ** p<0.05, * p<0.1.

2-digit NAICS industry controls included in regressions. Coefficients not shown.

Perhaps more interesting is the next set of regressions. In this logistic model, the dependent variable is equal to one if the owner did not apply for credit at some point when he/she needed it for fear of having the loan application denied. This is the same wording of the question that was used in the various Surveys of Small Business Finances. In terms of credit constraints, we see clear evidence in the results from this model using the more recent Kauffman Firm Survey. In all four years, the coefficient on the minority dummy was positive and statistically significant, indicating that this group was more likely to fear having a loan denied than was their White counterpart group, even after controlling for other factors, such as creditworthiness, industry, legal form, etc. This is perhaps the clearest recent evidence of continued borrowing constraints for Black and Hispanic business owners in the United States. Women were also more likely than men to have this fear during the economic crisis. Although the coefficient was positive in all four years, there was no statistically significant difference in the pre-crisis year of 2007 for women. There was no difference between high tech and non-high tech firms in any of the years.

However, being creditworthy, as indicated by a high credit score, was associated with lower incidences of fearing a loan application would be denied. Interestingly, the main human capital variable that factored in was previous startup experience, which was actually positively associated with the fear. A possible interpretation of this result is that previous startup experience may have resulted in business closure or failure, which is not captured in the survey but is likely known to banks. Logically, having started a business that failed in the past might lead to lower likelihood of new loan approvals and a greater fear of being denied.

Table 7. Did Not Apply for Credit When Needed for Fear of Having Loan Application Denied

VARIABLES	2007	2008	2009	2010
Black/ Hispanic	0.966***	1.101***	0.977***	1.123***
	(0.176)	(0.171)	(0.182)	(0.184)
Asian	-0.229	0.320	0.439	0.519*
	(0.366)	(0.338)	(0.310)	(0.315)
Female	0.237	0.316**	0.345**	0.346**
	(0.165)	(0.161)	(0.164)	(0.168)
High Tech	-0.163	0.240	-0.0313	0.253
	(0.254)	(0.240)	(0.239)	(0.233)
High Credit Score	-0.839***	-0.611**	-0.413	-0.295
	(0.272)	(0.257)	(0.256)	(0.261)
Medium Credit Score	-0.193	-0.123	-0.0523	-0.197
	(0.157)	(0.158)	(0.162)	(0.168)
Incorporated	0.206	0.296*	0.319*	0.390**
	(0.157)	(0.156)	(0.163)	(0.176)
Intellectual Property	-0.0275	0.0228	0.126	-0.0430
	(0.183)	(0.181)	(0.170)	(0.185)
Product Offering(s)	0.106	0.203	0.0986	-0.0263
	(0.170)	(0.162)	(0.160)	(0.168)
Home Based	-0.179	-0.0380	-0.0992	-0.182
	(0.150)	(0.149)	(0.151)	(0.159)

Table 7. (Continued)

VARIABLES	2007	2008	2009	2010
Hours Worked	0.0166***	0.0114***	0.0154***	0.00889***
	(0.00340)	(0.00303)	(0.00316)	(0.00317)
Industry Experience	-0.00434	-0.00245	-0.0174**	-0.0101
	(0.00808)	(0.00800)	(0.00759)	(0.00809)
Age	-0.0632	-0.0309	-0.00806	0.113**
	(0.0462)	(0.0467)	(0.0479)	(0.0560)
Team Ownership	-0.203	-0.538***	-0.229	-0.280
	(0.171)	(0.174)	(0.167)	(0.179)
Age Squared	0.000472	0.000152	1.64e-05	-0.00135**
	(0.000506)	(0.000508)	(0.000517)	(0.000616)
Some College	0.0969	0.264	-0.0138	0.264
	(0.240)	(0.242)	(0.240)	(0.253)
College Degree	-0.299	-0.101	-0.287	-0.0882
	(0.256)	(0.257)	(0.255)	(0.270)
Graduate Degree+	-0.218	0.0778	-0.224	-0.236
	(0.290)	(0.297)	(0.281)	(0.298)
Startup Experience	0.341**	0.251*	0.201	0.372**
	(0.145)	(0.146)	(0.144)	(0.150)
Constant	-0.538	-1.287	-1.456	-4.135***
	(1.099)	(1.111)	(1.129)	(1.328)
Observations	2,725	2,436	2,168	1,956

Excluded dummies: White, High School Degree or Less, Low Credit Score Standard errors in parentheses.
*** $p<0.01$, ** $p<0.05$, * $p<0.1$.
2-digit NAICS industry controls included in regressions. Coefficients not shown.

In terms of loan application outcomes, there is also strong evidence of credit constraints among Black- and Hispanic-owned businesses. Even after controlling for other factors, such as credit score, legal form, etc., the minority group made up of Black and Hispanic business owners was significantly less likely to have their loan applications approved, compared with their White counterparts. In fact, the magnitude increased dramatically over the period and through the crisis. Asians were not statistically different from Whites. Females were less likely to be approved in three of the four years, but the difference was statistically significant only in 2008. As expected, having a high credit score was positively correlated with having the loan application approved in three of the four years and was highly significant in 2008. The coefficient on high tech was negative in three of the four years, but it was never statistically significant in any of the years. The other results were mixed, but having intellectual property was negatively correlated with loan application approval in three of the four years, but was never statistically significant. Previous industry experience was positively associated with approval, but statistically significant only in one of the four years. Startup experience did factor in again in this model, being negatively associated with loan approvals in three of the four years and statistically significant in two of those three years.

Table 8. Loan Application(s) Always Approved

VARIABLES	2007	2008	2009	2010
Black/ Hispanic	-1.403***	-1.669***	-1.923***	-2.799***
	(0.501)	(0.614)	(0.547)	(0.827)
Asian	1.063	-0.657	-0.640	-1.566**
	(0.932)	(0.820)	(0.871)	(0.689)
Female	-0.208	-1.117***	-0.253	0.0201
	(0.460)	(0.430)	(0.427)	(0.562)
High Tech	-0.895	-0.544	-0.209	0.206
	(0.591)	(0.549)	(0.598)	(0.906)
High Credit Score	0.702	1.834***	0.126	-0.209
	(0.614)	(0.611)	(0.556)	(0.656)
Medium Credit Score	-0.270	0.316	-0.550	0.635
	(0.405)	(0.431)	(0.450)	(0.544)
Incorporated	-0.429	-0.0319	0.140	-0.828
	(0.485)	(0.496)	(0.428)	(0.536)
Intellectual Property	-0.346	-0.403	-0.724*	0.0512
	(0.404)	(0.503)	(0.418)	(0.527)
Product Offering(s)	-0.0433	-0.107	-0.327	0.168
	(0.383)	(0.440)	(0.432)	(0.516)
Home Based	-0.103	0.605	-0.778*	-0.918*
	(0.427)	(0.427)	(0.401)	(0.487)
Hours Worked	-0.00893	-0.0160	0.00171	-0.00441
	(0.00865)	(0.00988)	(0.00764)	(0.00995)
Industry Experience	4.80e-05	0.0121	0.0282	0.0567**

Table 8. (Continued)

VARIABLES	2007	2008	2009	2010
	(0.0213)	(0.0210)	(0.0191)	(0.0276)
Age	0.0422	0.144	0.123	-0.182
	(0.149)	(0.145)	(0.149)	(0.238)
Team Ownership	-0.0356	0.148	0.0723	0.151
	(0.410)	(0.418)	(0.364)	(0.451)
Age Squared	2.45e-05	-0.000883	-0.00124	0.00240
	(0.00166)	(0.00161)	(0.00160)	(0.00285)
Some College	1.066	1.237*	0.490	0.296
	(0.683)	(0.659)	(0.712)	(0.730)
College Degree	1.089	0.650	-0.274	-0.0985
	(0.739)	(0.609)	(0.709)	(0.690)
Graduate Degree+	1.043	-0.133	0.199	0.292
	(0.859)	(0.683)	(0.685)	(0.809)
Startup Experience	-0.540	-0.793**	0.167	-1.123**
	(0.397)	(0.387)	(0.362)	(0.512)
Constant	-0.201	-3.587	-2.796	4.527
	(3.268)	(3.195)	(3.497)	(5.072)
Observations	676	568	415	208

Excluded dummies: White, High School Degree or Less, Low Credit Score Standard errors in parentheses.
*** p<0.01, ** p<0.05, * p<0.1.
2-digit NAICS industry controls included in regressions. Coefficients not shown.

The results from the model on not applying for credit when needed for fear of denial as well as the model on loan approval provide evidence that Black- and Hispanic-owned businesses face greater credit constraints at startup and on an ongoing basis than do their White and Asian counterparts. The last two sets of regressions look at the levels of financial capital and the ratio of outsider debt to total financing.

In terms of the levels of financial capital injected at each year, the results indicate that even when controlling for other factors, including credit score, we still generally find Blacks, Hispanics, and women using lower levels of financial capital at startup, but that these differences do not continue over time conditional on survival to that period. The coefficient on the minority dummy was negative and statistically significant in the startup year, but not in the years 2007-2010. The coefficient on female was generally negative, but statistically significant only in two of the four follow-up years. High tech firms were generally more likely to have higher levels of financial capital invested, but the difference was statistically significant only in two of the six years. Having a high credit score was positive and statistically significant at startup, but not for follow-up years. Being incorporated and having intellectual property were generally positively associated with higher levels of financial capital investments, as were average hours worked and offering a product (as compared with service offerings). Being home based was negatively associated with higher levels of financial capital.

So the evidence suggests that, after controlling for credit quality, industry, and other owner and firm characteristics, the racial and gender differences in levels of financial capital are generally not statistically significant in subsequent years with only a couple of exceptions. By the time we collected owner wealth in the dataset, it didn't appear to change our findings in terms of levels of financial capital invested.

Table 9. Log of Total Financial Capital Invested

VARIABLES	2004	2007	2008	2009	2009 w/wealth	2010
High Wealth ($250K+)					0.0447	
					(0.297)	
Black/ Hispanic	-0.362**	0.0327	-0.182	-0.137	-0.0706	0.0779
	(0.162)	(0.341)	(0.356)	(0.388)	(0.417)	(0.373)
Asian	0.373	0.0292	0.194	0.444	0.348	0.414
	(0.265)	(0.634)	(0.656)	(0.645)	(0.691)	(0.646)
Female	-0.103	-0.520*	-0.216	-0.506*	-0.268	-0.0191
	(0.135)	(0.273)	(0.275)	(0.290)	(0.310)	(0.301)
High Tech	0.823***	0.465	0.785*	0.583	0.291	0.699
	(0.230)	(0.432)	(0.418)	(0.447)	(0.481)	(0.458)
High Credit Score	0.556***	0.216	0.0483	0.0459	-0.0729	0.145
	(0.138)	(0.264)	(0.274)	(0.290)	(0.308)	(0.296)
Medium Credit Score	-0.298	-0.161	-0.164	-0.0935	-0.0621	0.180
	(0.213)	(0.410)	(0.422)	(0.420)	(0.443)	(0.413)
Incorporated	0.753***	0.411	0.657**	1.050***	1.062***	0.866***
	(0.137)	(0.278)	(0.270)	(0.286)	(0.308)	(0.297)
Intellectual Property	0.0976	0.525*	0.502*	0.420	0.243	0.432

Table 9. (Continued)

VARIABLES	2004	2007	2008	2009	2009 w/wealth	2010
	(0.151)	(0.293)	(0.298)	(0.309)	(0.337)	(0.331)
Product Offering(s)	0.434***	0.990***	0.738***	0.859***	0.901***	0.597**
	(0.143)	(0.274)	(0.277)	(0.291)	(0.310)	(0.297)
Home Based	-0.820***	-0.389	-0.676**	-0.797***	-0.770***	-0.488*
	(0.137)	(0.253)	(0.265)	(0.278)	(0.298)	(0.283)
Hours Worked	0.0349***	0.0307***	0.0255***	0.0202***	0.0213***	0.0219***
	(0.00283)	(0.00520)	(0.00533)	(0.00566)	(0.00604)	(0.00571)
Industry Experience	-0.0316***	-0.00182	-0.00366	-0.00657	-0.0112	-0.00754
	(0.00670)	(0.0126)	(0.0126)	(0.0131)	(0.0140)	(0.0138)
Age	0.0550	-0.0732	-0.124*	0.0279	0.0585	0.0198
	(0.0365)	(0.0717)	(0.0736)	(0.0817)	(0.0879)	(0.0849)
Team Ownership	0.529***	0.425	0.0804	0.612**	0.411	0.487
	(0.146)	(0.299)	(0.292)	(0.311)	(0.337)	(0.323)
Age Squared	-0.000393	0.000810	0.00131*	-0.000179	-0.000469	2.83e-05
	(0.000398)	(0.000753)	(0.000775)	(0.000859)	(0.000925)	(0.000905)
Some College	-0.0136	0.207	0.151	0.771*	0.654	0.374
	(0.187)	(0.407)	(0.408)	(0.433)	(0.463)	(0.439)
College Degree	-0.111	0.135	0.0680	0.978**	0.899*	-0.122
	(0.207)	(0.427)	(0.430)	(0.448)	(0.482)	(0.463)
Graduate Degree+	0.108	0.372	-0.350	0.872*	0.761	-0.648
	(0.230)	(0.468)	(0.481)	(0.498)	(0.540)	(0.510)
Startup Experience	0.0398	0.549**	0.444*	0.0219	0.0885	0.429
	(0.125)	(0.240)	(0.246)	(0.260)	(0.277)	(0.271)
Constant	5.173***	6.297***	8.496***	2.949	2.355	2.445
	(0.884)	(1.776)	(1.816)	(2.014)	(2.163)	(2.053)
Observations	3,744	2,406	2,295	2,114	1,883	1,959
R-squared	0.173	0.088	0.074	0.087	0.074	0.065

Excluded dummies: White, High School Degree or Less, Low Credit Score Standard errors in parentheses.
*** $p<0.01$, ** $p<0.05$, * $p<0.1$.
2-digit NAICS industry controls included in regressions. Coefficients not shown.

In terms of the ratio of outsider debt to total financing, we continue to see racial and gender differences. Blacks and Hispanics have much lower ratios of outsider debt, so they are relying less on formal financing channels such as bank financing, even after controlling for other factors, most notably creditworthiness and wealth levels. There were not statistically significant differences for female ownership, compared with male ownership, although the coefficient was negative in all of the years. As we saw in the univariate statistics, women used much lower levels of financial capital, but weren't very different from men in terms of the share of the financing that came from outside debt financing. Thus, it's not too surprising that there were no significant differences after controlling for other factors.

Interestingly, high tech firms were actually more reliant on outsider debt, controlling for other factors. This was the case at startup and in subsequent years. High credit score mattered in the early years, but not so much in the latter years. Incorporated firms were more reliant on outsider debt, as were older owners that worked more hours. Home-based firms and firms with product offerings were less reliant on outsider debt. Other owner variables such as education and startup experience didn't play any role in the ratio of outsider debt to total financial capital invested. Firms with intellectual property were less reliant on outsider debt, again consistent with findings from Robb and Seamans (2012) and Robb and Winston-Smith (2012), who found that more complex and informationally opaque firms relied more on equity financing than debt financing.

These findings were also robust to including controls for growth expectations (available only in 2008) and additional controls for firm size, employment growth, and revenue growth.

Table 10. Ratio of Outsider Debt to Total Financial Capital Invested

VARIABLES	2004	2007	2008	2009	2009 w/ wealth	2010	2010 w/ wealth
High Wealth ($250K+)					0.0835***		0.137***
					(0.0309)		(0.0340)
Black/ Hispanic	-0.0622***	-0.100***	-0.117***	-0.122***	-0.127***	-0.136***	-0.110**
	(0.0151)	(0.0349)	(0.0347)	(0.0401)	(0.0426)	(0.0433)	(0.0448)
Asian	-0.00494	-0.00429	0.0832	-0.0884	-0.0823	-0.112	-0.0881
	(0.0337)	(0.0673)	(0.0703)	(0.0677)	(0.0703)	(0.0695)	(0.0696)
Female	-0.00543	-0.0331	-0.0219	-0.0453	-0.0501	-0.0376	-0.0563
	(0.0145)	(0.0307)	(0.0294)	(0.0327)	(0.0346)	(0.0351)	(0.0361)
High Tech	0.0695***	0.158***	0.109**	0.168***	0.138***	0.107**	0.117**
	(0.0233)	(0.0433)	(0.0427)	(0.0460)	(0.0498)	(0.0501)	(0.0527)
High Credit Score	0.0350***	0.0497*	0.0298	0.0382	0.0234	0.0279	0.0193
	(0.0136)	(0.0291)	(0.0291)	(0.0319)	(0.0333)	(0.0353)	(0.0370)

Table 10. (Continued)

VARIABLES	2004	2007	2008	2009	2009 w/ wealth	2010	2010 w/ wealth
Medium Credit Score	-0.0550***	-0.0225	-0.0213	-0.00531	-0.00829	0.00171	0.000747
	(0.0185)	(0.0420)	(0.0422)	(0.0482)	(0.0504)	(0.0512)	(0.0546)
Incorporated	0.0452***	0.128***	0.143***	0.127***	0.113***	0.108***	0.0909**
	(0.0142)	(0.0300)	(0.0296)	(0.0317)	(0.0335)	(0.0350)	(0.0370)
Intellectual Property	-0.0198	-0.102***	-0.0597*	-0.0708**	-0.0938**	-0.0484	-0.0903**
	(0.0151)	(0.0307)	(0.0310)	(0.0340)	(0.0366)	(0.0363)	(0.0381)
Product Offering(s)	0.0239*	-0.0485*	-0.0468*	0.0207	0.00437	-0.0782**	-0.100***
	(0.0144)	(0.0293)	(0.0283)	(0.0310)	(0.0335)	(0.0332)	(0.0349)
Home Based	-0.0413***	-0.0392	-0.0442	-0.0144	-0.0298	-0.0815**	-0.0861**
	(0.0134)	(0.0269)	(0.0273)	(0.0293)	(0.0311)	(0.0337)	(0.0353)
Hours Worked	0.000593**	0.000921*	0.00115**	0.00106*	0.00165***	0.000441	0.000785
	(0.000268)	(0.000554)	(0.000553)	(0.000594)	(0.000628)	(0.000666)	(0.000701)
Industry Experience	-0.00105	-0.00256*	0.000732	-0.00103	-0.00196	0.000402	-0.000848
	(0.000684)	(0.00131)	(0.00133)	(0.00143)	(0.00147)	(0.00158)	(0.00161)
Age	0.00640*	0.0159**	0.0131*	0.0284***	0.0298***	0.0104	0.0111
	(0.00353)	(0.00720)	(0.00784)	(0.00818)	(0.00889)	(0.00959)	(0.0103)
Team Ownership	0.0167	-0.0157	0.0636**	0.0475	0.0320	0.0154	0.0152
	(0.0148)	(0.0308)	(0.0306)	(0.0319)	(0.0340)	(0.0347)	(0.0372)
Age Squared	-5.80e-05	-0.000167**	-0.000152*	-0.000338*** -0.000361	***	-0.000161	-0.000181*
	(3.77e-05)	(7.41e-05)	(8.30e-05)	(8.47e-05)	(9.19e-05)	(0.000101)	(0.000109)
Some College	-0.00529	0.0585	0.0769*	-0.0182	-0.0138	-0.0231	-0.0362
	(0.0200)	(0.0396)	(0.0410)	(0.0508)	(0.0536)	(0.0543)	(0.0577)
College Degree	-0.0175	0.0338	0.0965**	-0.0316	-0.0518	0.00263	-0.0217
	(0.0215)	(0.0415)	(0.0425)	(0.0520)	(0.0552)	(0.0552)	(0.0590)
Graduate Degree+	0.00620	0.0147	0.0457	-0.0277	-0.0439	0.0220	-0.0153
	(0.0243)	(0.0459)	(0.0486)	(0.0558)	(0.0594)	(0.0598)	(0.0644)
Startup Experience	0.00681	0.00857	-0.0383	0.00995	0.0113	0.0113	0.0366
	(0.0130)	(0.0261)	(0.0261)	(0.0285)	(0.0301)	(0.0309)	(0.0321)
Constant	-0.00233	0.0943	0.0874	-0.133	-0.131	0.364	0.409
	(0.0850)	(0.181)	(0.190)	(0.202)	(0.223)	(0.242)	(0.259)

VARIABLES	2004	2007	2008	2009	2009 w/ wealth	2010	2010 w/ wealth
Observations	3,363	1,628	1,540	1,305	1,166	1,115	967
R-squared	0.054	0.091	0.122	0.120	0.137	0.097	0.143

Excluded dummies: White, High School Degree or Less, Low Credit Scor   Standard
    errors in parentheses.
*** p<0.01, ** p<0.05, * p<0.1.
2-digit NAICS industry controls included in regressions. Coefficients not shown.

CONCLUSION

Key findings of this study include the fact that firms owned by African Americans and Hispanics utilize a different mix of equity and debt capital, relative to firms owned by nonminorities. Relying disproportionately upon owner equity investments and employing relatively less debt from outside sources (primarily banks), the mean firm in these minority business subgroups operates with substantially less capital overall – both at startup and in subsequent years – relative to their nonminority counterparts. Women-owned businesses exhibit some similar disparities in capital structure, relative to male-owned firms, in the sense of operating with much less capital, on average, and a somewhat different mix of debt and equity capital. Their reliance upon outside equity capital is particularly low. The initial disparities in the levels of startup capital by gender do not disappear in the subsequent years following startup, but are generally explained in most years by differences in other firm characteristics.

The multivariate findings indicate that among new and young firms, women were no more or less likely to apply for new loans than men. However, minorities were less likely than their White counterparts to apply for new loans when their firms were in the early years of operation. The analysis also suggests that minority owners who did not apply for new loans were significantly more likely than their White counterparts to avoid applying for loans when needed because they were afraid that their loan applications would be declined by lenders. This is even after controlling for credit quality and a host of owner and firm characteristics. Women were also more likely than similar men not to apply for credit when it was needed for fear of having their loan application denied during the years of the economic crisis.

The analysis showed that women and minority business owners' fears of being declined for a loan were not necessarily unwarranted. In particular, in terms of loan application outcomes, even after controlling for such factors as industry, credit score, legal form, and human capital, minority owners of young firms were significantly less likely to have their loan applications approved than were similar White business owners. Similarly, in 2008, women owners of new businesses were significantly less likely than men with similar credit profiles and legal forms of organization to be approved for loans. More generally, the results suggest that in the initial year of startup, Black- and Hispanic-owned businesses faced greater credit constraints than did their White and Asian counterparts. Similarly, women-owned businesses faced greater credit constraints than did similar startups owned by men during the years of the financial crisis.

In terms of the levels of financial capital, however, the evidence suggests that, after controlling for credit quality, industry, and other owner and firm characteristics, racial differences were generally not statistically significant, while in two of the years of observation, women used lower levels of financial capital. Finally, the results suggested that Blacks and Hispanics relied less than Whites on formal financing channels such as bank financing, even after controlling for creditworthiness and wealth levels. However, women-owned startups were not significantly different from those owned by men in terms of the share of their financing that came from outside debt financing.

As expected, high tech firms generally had higher levels of financial capital than their non- high tech counterparts. Surprisingly, however, they were actually more reliant on formal debt financing than were similar firms that were not high tech in nature. This was true both at startup and in subsequent years before and during the recent financial crisis. Having intellectual property however, was negatively associated with greater reliance on formal debt financing. This may indicate that the kinds of high tech firms that rely on patents, trademarks, and copyrights to protect their intellectual property are more informationally opaque and therefore less attractive as borrowers for bank financing, rather than just high tech firms more generally. Indeed, in three of the four years the coefficient on intellectual property was negative in the equation for loan approvals and in two of those years the difference was statistically significant.

While this study is limited in that it is focused on one cohort of firms that began operations in 2004, it documents significant racial and gender disparities in capital access, as well as differences in financing patterns by high tech and non-high tech firms. It is hoped that these findings will help policymakers in developing policies to ensure optimal access to debt and equity capital among all small businesses, especially during tough economic times and among those that have been disadvantaged historically in financial markets.

REFERENCES

Ahl, Helene. 2006. "Why Research on Women Entrepreneurs Needs New Directions." *Entrepreneurship Theory and Practice*, 30: 595–621.

Allen, W. David. 2000. "Social Networks and Self-Employment," *Journal of Socio-Economics*, 487-501.

Astebro, Thomas and Irwin Bernhardt. 2003. "Start-Up Financing, Owner Characteristics and Survival," *Journal of Economics and Business*, 303-320.

Avery, Robert B., Raphael W. Bostic, and Katherine A. Samolyk. 1998. "The Role of Personal Wealth in Small Business Finance," *Journal of Banking and Finance*, 1019-1061.

Ayyagari, Meghana, Asli Demirguc-Kunt, and Vojislav Maksimovic. 2010. "Formal Versus Informal Finance: Evidence from China." Review of Financial Studies 23(8): 3048-3097.

Bates, Timothy and David Howell. 1997. "The Declining Status of African American Men in the New York City Construction Industry, *Race, Markets, and Social Outcomes*, ed. Patrick Mason and Rhonda Williams. Boston: Kluwer.

Bates, Timothy and William Bradford. 2007. "Traits and Performance of the Minority Venture Capital Industry." *Annals of the American Academy of Political and Social Science* 613(3): 95-107.

Bates, Timothy and William D. Bradford. 2008. "Venture-Capital Investment in Minority Business," *Journal of Money Credit and Banking*, March/April: 489-504.

Bates, Timothy, and David Blanchflower. 2007. *Analysis of the Role of Businesses Owned by Minorities and Women in the Procurement Activities of the Metropolitan Pier and Exposition Authority*. Report to the Metropolitan Pier and Exposition Authority.

Bates, Timothy. 1993. *Banking on Black Enterprise* (Washington, D.C.: Joint Center for Political and Economic Studies.

Bates, Timothy. 1997. *Race, Self-Employment & Upward Mobility: An Elusive American Dream.* Washington, D.C.: Woodrow Wilson Center Press and Baltimore: John Hopkins University Press.

Bates, Timothy. 1998. *Discrimination and the Capacity of Chicago-Area Minority-Owned Businesses to Participate in Public Procurement: Report to the City of Chicago Department of Law.*

Bates, Timothy. 2002. "Restricted Access to Markets Characterizes Women-Owned Businesses," *Journal of Business Venturing,* 17: 313-24.

Bates, Timothy. 2005. "Financing Disadvantaged Firms." *Credit Markets for the Poor,* ed. Patrick Bolton and Howard Rosenthal. Russell Sage Foundation, 149-178.

Beck, Thorsten, Asli Demirgüç-Kunt, Vojislav Maksimovic. 2008.Financing patterns around the world: Are small firms different. *Journal of Financial Economics,* Volume 89, Issue 3.467- 487.

Becker, Gary.1971. The Economics of Discrimination. Chicago: University of Chicago Press.

Becker-Blease, John R., and Jeffrey E. Sohl. 2007. "Do Women-Owned Businesses Have Equal Access to Angel Capital?" *Journal of Business Venturing* 22 (4): 503–21.

Becker-Blease, John R., Susan Elkinawy, and March Stater. 2010. "The Impact of Gender of Voluntary and Involuntary Executive Departure." *Economic Inquiry* 48 (4): 1102–18.

Black, Jane, David de Meza, and David Jeffreys. 1996. "House Prices,The Supply of Collateral and the Enterprise Economy," *The Economic Journal,* 60-75.

Black, Sandra E., and Philip E. Strahan, 2002, Entrepreneurship and bank credit availability, Journal of Finance 57, 2807-2833."

Blanchard, Lloyd, John Yinger and Bo Zhao. 2004. "Do Credit Market Barriers Exist for Minority and Women Entrepreneurs?" Syracuse University Working Paper.

Blanchflower, David. 2007. *Entrepreneurship in the United States,* IZA working paper No. 3130

Blanchflower, David G., P. Levine and D. Zimmerman. 2003. "Discrimination in the small business credit market", *Review of Economics and Statistics,* November, 85(4), pp. 930-943.

Blanchflower, David G. and Andrew J. Oswald. 1998. "What Makes and Entrepreneur?," *Journal of Labor Economics,* January: 26-60.

Bobbitt-Zeher, Donna. 2007. "The Gender Income Gap and the Role of Education." Sociology of Education 80 (1): 1–22.

Boden, Richard. 1996. "Gender and Self-Employment Selection: An Empirical Assessment," *Journal of Socio-Economics,* 25(6), pp. 671-682.

Boden, Richard J. Jr., and Alfred R. Nucci. 2000. "On the Survival Prospects of Men's and Women's New Business Ventures." *Journal of Business Venturing* 15 (4): 347–62.

Borjas, George and Stephen Bronars. 1989. "Consumer Discrimination and Self-Employment." *Journal of Political Economy*, 581-605.

Bostic, R. and K.P. Lampani. 1999. "Racial Differences in Patterns of Small Business Finance: The Importance of Local Geography," Working Paper.

Brush, Candida. 1997. "Women-Owned Businesses: Obstacles and Opportunities," *Journal of Developmental Entrepreneurship*. 2: 1-24.

Brush, Candida. 1998. "A Resource Perspective on Women's Entrepreneurship," in *Women Entrepreneurs in Small and Medium Enterprises*. Paris: Organization for Economic Cooperation and Development.

Brush, Candida G., Nancy M. Carter, Patricia G. Greene, Myra M. Hart, and Elizabeth Gatewood. 2002. "The Role of Social Capital and Gender in Linking Financial Suppliers and Entrepreneurial Firms: A Framework for Future Research." Venture Capital 4 (4): 305–23.

Caballero, Ricardo J. and Arvind Krishnamurthy. 2008. "Collective Risk Management in a Flight to Quality Episode." The Journal of Finance 63:2195–2230.

Cagetti, Marco, and Mariacristina De Nardi, 2006. "Entrepreneurship, frictions, and wealth, *Journal of Political Economy* 114, 835-870."

Carter, Nancy M., Mary Williams, and Paul D. Reynolds. 1997. "Discontinuance Among New Firms in Retail: The Influence of Initial Resources, Strategy, and Gender." *Journal of Business Venturing* 12: 125–45.

Cavalluzzo, Ken and John Wolken. 2005. "Small Business Loan Turndowns, Personal Wealth and Discrimination," *Journal of Business*, 2153-2177.

Cavalluzzo, Ken, Linda Cavalluzzo, and John Wolken. 2002. "Competition, Small Business Financing, and Discrimination: Evidence from a New Survey." *The Journal of Business* 75 (4): 641–79.

Chava, Sudheer and Amiyatosh Purnanandam. 2011. "The Effect of Banking Crisis on Bank-Dependent Borrowers." *Journal of Financial Economics* 99(1): 116-135."

Cliff, Jennifer E. 1998. "Does One Size Fit All? Exploring the Relationship Between Attitudes Toward Growth, Gender, and Business Size." *Journal of Business Venturing* 13: 523–42.

Coleman, Susan. 2002. "The Borrowing Experience of Black and Hispanic-Owned Small Firms: Evidence from the 1998 Survey of Small Business Finances," *The Academy of Entrepreneurship Journal 8*: 1-20.

Coleman, Susan. 2003. "Borrowing Patterns for Small Firms: A Comparison by Race and Ethnicity." *The Journal of Entrepreneurial Finance & Business Ventures 7*: 87-108.

Coleman, Susan, and Alicia M. Robb. 2009. "A Comparison of New Firm Financing by Gender: Evidence from the Kauffman Firm Survey Data." Small Business Economics 33: 397–411. Constantinidis, Christina, Annie Cornet, and Simona Asandei. 2006. "Financing of Women-Owned Ventures: The Impact of Gender and Other Owner- and Firm- Related Variables." *Venture Capital* 8 (2): 133–57.

Dunn, Thomas and Douglas Holtz-Eakin., Michael and Harvey S. Rosen. 2000. "Self-Employment, Family Background, and Race," *Journal of Human Resources*, (2000): 670-692.

Dunn, Thomas A. and Douglas J. Holtz-Eakin. 2000. "Financial Capital, Human Capital, and the Transition to Self-Employment: Evidence from Intergenerational Links," *Journal of Labor Economics*, 282-305.

Earle, John S. and Zuzana Sakova. 2000. "Business start-ups or disguised unemployment? Evidence on the character of self-employment from transition economies," *Labour Economics*, 575– 601.

Edelstein, Robert H. 1975. "Improving the selection of credit risks: An analysis of a commercial bank minority lending program," The *Journal of Finance* 30, 37-55."

Evans, David S. and Boyan Jovanovic. 1989. "An Estimated Model of Entrepreneurial Choice under Liquidity Constraints," *Journal of Political Economy*, 808-827.

Evans, David S. and Linda S. Leighton. 1989. "Some Empirical Aspects of Entrepreneurship," *American Economic Review*, (June): 519-535.

Fairlie, Robert W. 1999. "The Absence of the African-American Owned Business: An Analysis of the Dynamics of Self-Employment," *Journal of Labor Economics*, 80-108.

Fairlie, Robert W. 2006. "Entrepreneurship among Disadvantaged Groups: An Analysis of the Dynamics of Self-Employment by Gender, Race and Education," *The Life Cycle of Entrepreneurial Ventures, International Handbook Series on Entrepreneurship , Vol. 3*, ed. Simon Parker. Springer: New York.

Fairlie, Robert W. 2008. Estimating the Contribution of Immigrant Business Owners to the U.S. Economy, Final Report for U.S. Small Business Administration.

Fairlie, Robert W., and Alicia M. Robb. 2009. "Gender Differences in Business Performance: Evidence from the Characteristics of Business Owners Survey." *Small Business Economics* 33: 375–95.

Fairlie, Robert W. and Alicia M. Robb. 2008. *Race and Entrepreneurial Success: Black-, Asian-, and White-Owned Businesses in the United States.* Cambridge, MA: The MIT Press.

Fairlie, Robert W. and Alicia M. Robb. 2007. "Why are Black-Owned Businesses Less Successful then White-Owned Businesses: The Role of Families, Inheritances, and Business Human Capital," *Journal of Labor Economics,* 289-323.

Fairlie, Robert W. and Christopher Woodruff. 2009. "Mexican-American Entrepreneurship." University of California Working Paper.

Fairlie, Robert W. and Harry A. Krashinsky. 2008. "Liquidity Constraints, Household Wealth, and Entrepreneurship Revisited," Working Paper.

Fairlie, Robert W., and Bruce D. Meyer. 1996. "Ethnic and Racial Self-Employment Differences and Possible Explanations," *Journal of Human Resources*, 31, Fall 1996, pp. 757-793.

Fairlie, Robert W., Julie Zissimopoulos, and Harry Krashinsky. 2008. "The International Asian Business Success Story? A Comparison of Chinese, Indian and Other Asian Businesses in the United States, Canada and United Kingdom," NBER Volume on International Differences in Entrepreneurship.

Feagin, Joe R., and Nikitah Imani. 1994. "Racial barriers to African American entrepreneurship: an exploratory study," *Social Problems*, November, 41(4): 562-585.

Gertler, Mark and Simon Gilchrist. 1994. "Monetary Policy, Business Cycles, and the Behavior of Small Manufacturing Firms," Quarterly Journal of Economics 109(2):309-340.

Gorton, Gary and Andrew Winton, 2003, Financial Intermediation, in The Handbook of the Economics of Finance: Corporate Finance, edited by George Constantinides, Milton Harris, and Rene Stulz (Elsevier Science; 2003) (NBER Working Paper # 8928).

Greenhalgh, Paul. 2008. "An Examination of Business Occupier Relocation Decision Making: Distinguishing Small and Large Firm Behaviour." *Journal of Property Research* 25(2): 107-126.

Haynes, George W. 2010. "Income and Wealth: How Did Households Owning Small Businesses Fare from 1998 to 2007?" Accessed at http://www.sba.gov/advo. U.S. Small Business Administration.

Holmstrom, Bengt., and Tirole, Jean. 1997 "Financial Intermediation, Loanable Funds, and The Real Sector." Quarterly Journal of Economics. Volume 112:Issue 3:663-691.

Holt, Colette. 2003. "Strict Constitutional Scrutiny is not Fatal in Fact: Federal Courts Uphold Affirmative Action Programs in Public Contracting." *CCH Labor Law Journal* 54: 248-262.

Holtz-Eakin, Douglas and Harvey S. Rosen. 2005. "Cash Constraints and Business Start-Ups: Deutschmarks versus Dollars," *Contributions to Economic Analysis & Policy*.

Holtz-Eakin, Douglas, David Joulfaian and Harvey S. Rosen. 1994. "Entrepreneurial Decisions and Liquidity Constraints," *RAND Journal of Economics*, (Summer): 334-347.

Hout, Michael and Harvey S. Rosen. 1999. "Self-Employment, Family Background, and Race." *NBER Working Paper* 7344.

Ivashina, Victoria and David Scharfstein. 2010. "Loan Syndication and Credit Cycles." American Economic Review.

Johansson, Edward. 2000. "Self-employment and Liquidity Constraints: Evidence from Finland," *Scandinavian Journal of Economics,* 123-134.

Kawaguchi, Daiji. 2005. "Negative Self Selection into Self-Employment among African Americans," *Topics in Economic Analysis & Policy, Berkeley Electronic Press Journals*, 1- 25.

Kerr, Willam and Nanda, Ramana. 2009. "Financing Constraints and Entrepreneurship." *NBER Working Paper* No. 15498

Kim, Kwang, Won Hurh, and Maryilyn Fernandez. 1989. "Intragroup Differences in Business Participation: Three Asian Immigrant Groups," *International Migration Review* 23(1),

Lentz, Bernard and David Laband. 1999. "Entrepreneurial Success and Occupational Inheritance among Proprietors," *Canadian Journal of Economics*, 563-579.

Lindh, Thomas and Henry Ohlsson. 1996. "Self-Employment and Windfall Gains: Evidence from the Swedish Lottery," *Economic Journal*, (November): 1515-1526.

Lofstrom , Magnus and Timothy Bates. 2009. "Latina Entrepreneurship." *Small Business Economics,*33:427-439.

Lofstrom, Magnus and Chunbei Wang, "Hispanic Self-Employment: A Dynamic Analysis of Business Ownership," University of Texas at Dallas Working Paper (2006).

Lusgarten, S. 1994. *Business ownership as an Employment Opportunity for Women.* Report to the U.S. Small Business Administration under contract # 8035-OA-93.

Mann, Ronald J. 1998. "Comment on Avery, Bostic and Samolyk." *Journal of Banking and Finance,* 22: 1062–66.

Mar, Don. 2005. "Individual Characteristics vs. City Structural Characteristics: Explaining Self-Employment Differences among Chinese, Japanese, and Filipinos in the United States," *Journal of Socio-Economics*, 34,

Marlow, Susan, and Dean Patton. 2005. "All Credit to Men? Entrepreneurship, Finance, and Gender." *Entrepreneurship Theory and Practice* 29 (3): 526–41.

Meyer, Bruce. 1990. "Why Are There So Few Black Entrepreneurs?," National Bureau of Economic Research, Working Paper No. 3537.

Mitchell, K. and D.K. Pearce. 2004. *Availability of Financing to Small Firms using the Survey of Small Business Finances.* United States Small Business Administration, Office of Advocacy.

Moon, John. 2009. "Small Business Finance and Personal Assets." Community Investments 21 (3): 9–10, 39.

Moutray, C. 2007. *Educational attainment and other characteristics of the self-employed: An examination using the Panel Study of Income Dynamics data.* U.S. Small Business Administration, Office of Advocacy, Working paper.

Nanda, Ramana, 2008, Cost of external finance and selection into entrepreneurship." Harvard Business School Working Paper 08-047."

National Center for Education Statistics Fast Facts, 2009. Degrees conferred by sex and race. http://nces.ed.gov/fastfacts/display.asp?id=72

National Science Foundation, ADVANCE Program. 2012. http://www.nsf.gov/funding/pgm_summ.jsp?pims_id=5383 accessed on 6/16/12

Orser, Barbara, and Sandra Hogarth-Scott. 2002. "Opting for Growth: Gender Dimensions of Choosing Enterprise Development." Canadian Journal of Administrative Sciences 19 (3): 284–300.

Parker, Simon C. 2004. *The Economics of Self-Employment and Entrepreneurship* (Cambridge: Cambridge University Press.

Robb, Alicia. 2002. "Entrepreneurship: A Path for Economic Advancement for Women and Minorities?," *Journal of Developmental Entrepreneurship,* Volume 7, No. 4.

Robb, Alicia, and Susan Coleman. 2010. "Financing Strategies of New Technology- Based Firms: A Comparison of Women-and Men-Owned Firms." Journal of Technology Management and Innovation 5 (1): 30–50.

Robb, Alicia and David Robinson.2012. "The Capital Structure Decisions of New Firms." *Review Of Financial Studies, Vol 1, No 1, 2012.*

Robb, Alicia and Robert Seamans, 2012. "Entrepreneurial Finance and Performance: A Transaction Cost Economics Approach," Working paper.

Robb, Alicia M., and John Wolken. 2002. "Firm, Owner, and Financing Characteristics: Differences between Female- and Male-Owned Small Businesses." Working Paper no. 2002-18, FEDS. http://www.federalreserve.gov/.

Robb, Alicia and Sheryl Winston-Smith. 2012. "Implications of Demand for and Access to Financial Capital by Young Firms in the Current Economic Crisis" Working paper.

Smith, Sheryl Winston. 2011. "Beg, Borrow, and Deal? Entrepreneurs' Choice of Financing and New Firm Innovation." Available at SSRN: http://ssrn.com/abstract=1573685 or http://dx.doi.org/10.2139/ssrn.1573685

Sohl, Jeffrey. "The Angel Investor Market in 2008: A Down Year In Investment Dollars But Not In Deals", Center for Venture Research, http://wsbe.unh.edu/ files/2008_ Analysis_ Report_Final.pdf. Accessed July 17, 2009.

Taylor, Mark P. 2001. "Self-Employment and Windfall Gains in Britain: Evidence from Panel Data," *Economica*, (November): 539-565.

U.S. Census Bureau, *1992 Economic Census: Characteristics of Business Owners.*

U.S. Census Bureau. 2009. Wealth and Asset Ownership, http://www.census.gov/hhes/www/wealth/2002/wlth02-2.html. Accessed July 29, 2009.

U.S Department of Commerce, Minority Business Development Agency, *The State of Minority Businesses.*

U.S. Department of Commerce, Minority Business Development Agency. 2006. *The State of Minority Business Enterprises, An Overview of the 2002 Survey of Business Owners, number of Firms, Gross Receipts, and Paid Employee.*

U.S. Department of Commerce, Minority Business Development Agency. 2008. *Characteristics of Minority Businesses and Entrepreneurs.*

U.S. Department of Commerce, Minority Business Development Agency. 2004. *Accelerating Job Creation and Economic Productivity: Expanding Financing Opportunities for Minority Businesses.*

U.S. Department of Commerce. 2008. Minority Business Development Agency, *Characteristics of Minority Businesses and Entrepreneurs.*

van der Sluis, J., M. van Praag and W. Vijverberg. 2004. *Education and Entrepreneurship in Industrialized Countries: A Meta-Analysis,* Tinbergen Institute Working Paper no. TI 03– 046/3 (Amsterdam: Tinbergen Institute, 2004).

Wainwright, Jon S. 2000. *Racial Discrimination and Minority Business Enterprise: Evidence from the 1990 Census.* Studies in Entrepreneurship Series. Edited by S. Bruchey. New York, Garland Publishing.

Wainwright, Jon S., Colette Holt, David Blanchflower, Deborah Norris, and Kim Stewart. 2006. *Race, Sex, and Business Enterprise: Evidence from Denver, Colorado.* Denver, Colorado.

Yago, Glenn and Aaron Pankrat. 2000. *The Minority Business Challenge: Democratizing Capital for Emerging Domestic Markets.* Milken Institute and the Minority Business Development Agency.

Zafar, Basit. 2009. "College Major Choice and the Gender Gap." Federal Reserve Bank of New York Staff Report no. 364.

APPENDIX: VARIABLE DEFINITIONS

High Wealth ($250K+)	Net wealth of $250,000 or more in 2008
Minority	Primary owner is black, Hispanic, or non-Asian other race
Asian	Primary owner is Asian
Female	Primary owner is female
High Tech	Technology based firm
High Credit Score	Credit score in the 71-100th percentile
Medium Credit Score	Credit score in the 31-70th percentile
Incorporated	Firm is incorporated as a C, S, or limited liability corporation
Intellectual Property	Firm has one or more patents, trademarks, and/or copyrigh
Product Offering(s)	Firm offers a product

	(versus a service, could offer both)
Home Based	Firm is based in the owner's home
Hours Worked	Average hours worked in a week
	by primary owner
Industry Experience	Previous years of industry experience
Age	Primary owner age
Team Ownership	Firm has two or more owners
Age Squared	Primary owner age squared
Some College	Primary owner has some college
College Degree	Primary owner has a college degree
Graduate Degree+	Primary owner has a graduate degree
Startup Experience	Primary owner has previous
	startup experience

End Note

[1] Lloyd Blanchard, John Yinger and Bo Zhao,"Do Credit Market Barriers Exist for Minority and Women Entrepreneurs?," Syracuse University Working Paper (2004). Blanchflower, Levine and Zimmerman. Cavalluzzo, Cavalluzzo, and Wolken. Cavalluzzo and Wolken. Susan Coleman,"The Borrowing Experience of Black and Hispanic-Owned Small Firms: Evidence from the 1998 Survey of Small Business Finances," *The Academy of Entrepreneurship Journal 8*, (2002): 1-20. Susan Coleman, "Borrowing Patterns for Small Firms: A Comparison by Race and Ethnicity." *The Journal of Entrepreneurial Finance & Business Ventures* 7, (2003): 87-108. United States Small Business Administration, Office of Advocacy, *Availability of Financing to Small Firms using the Survey of Small Business Finances*, K. Mitchell and D.K. Pearce, (2004).

In: Capital Access   ISBN: 978-1-62948-197-5
Editors: H. Drexler and G. Maines   © 2013 Nova Science Publishers, Inc.

Chapter 2

VENTURE CAPITAL, SOCIAL CAPITAL AND THE FUNDING OF WOMEN-LED BUSINESSES[*]

Small Business Administration, Office of Advocacy

EXECUTIVE SUMMARY

Studies of Women-Led Businesses (WLBs) have increased dramatically over the past 15 years. One consistent finding in this research is that WLBs receive less outside funding than Men-Led Businesses (MLBs). Further, Venture Capital (VC) funding of WLBs consisted of only 6% of the total funds invested in the United States between 1997 and 2000. Are there unique features to the VC firms that invest in WLBs? And how does investing in WLBs affect the subsequent performance of VC firms? Our study addresses these questions using a social capital lens.

Our data for this study consist of all U.S. VC investments from 2000 through 2010. The dataset includes 2,500 VC firms, 18,900 portfolio companies (those companies VC firms invested in during the 11 year period of the study), 92,500 individual management team members and 90,000

---

[*] This report, released April 2013, was produced by JMG Consulting, LLC and Wyckoff Consulting, LLC under a contract with the Small Business Administration, Office of Advocacy.

investment rounds. Using this data, we examine how the co-investing relationships among VC firms affect the funding of WLBs. We proposed that those VC firms without strong social capital, created through co-investing with other VC firms, would be more likely to invest in WLBs. Our results were mixed. VC firms that co-invest with other VC firms that do not co-invest with one another invest in a lower percentage of investments in WLBs. This social capital measure is called "structural holes." VC firms with lower rates of structural holes invest in a higher percentage of WLBs. Another finding is that VC firms that have longterm co-investing relationships with other VC firms that co-invest frequently with these other firms invest in a higher percentage of WLBs when compared to VC firms without long-term relationships. Finally, our study finds that the performance of VC firms improves as the ratio of investment in WLBs increases. This study provides insights for VC firms looking to improve their performance and to WLBs searching for VC funding.

INTRODUCTION

Research in women's entrepreneurship has increased during the past 15 years. One consistent finding in this research is that women-led businesses (WLBs) receive less funding than those companies led by men (MLB). Additionally, WLBs tend to be smaller and in slower growth industries. Studies examining the access to venture capital (VC) funding by WLBs have been limited, primarily due to lack of accurate and complete data. Further, most studies focus on aspects specific to the WLB, not the VC firm.

The first U.S. VC firm was established in 1946. VC funding remained quite small and stable until a significant increase in VC firms and funds occurred in the early 1980's. This increase was due, in part, to legal changes allowing pension funds to invest in venture capital. At the same time, the computer industry was experiencing substantial growth. These two factors created much of the growth in the nascent VC industry. Investment strategies of VC firms are categorized by investment stage and industry focus. Investment stage refers to the life-cycle stage of the portfolio company when the investment is made. Early stage investments are used as initial funding of start-ups, while later stage funding is available for product development and growth purposes. Additionally, VC firms may focus on a specific industry, such as telecommunications or computer hardware. VC firms commonly invest as a group, or syndicate, in entrepreneurial firms. A syndicate is created for each funding round of each portfolio company.

In this paper, we utilize a social capital lens to examine what factors influence VC firms' investments in WLBs. We utilize the definition of social capital, as "the sum of the actual and potential resources embedded within, available through and derived from the network of relationships possessed by an individual or social unit" as provided by Nahapiet and Ghoshal (1998: p. 243). Specifically, we use the three dimensions of social capital, structural, relational and cognitive. Structural social capital is who you know and how you know them. For example, the individuals you know at work are a part of your structural social capital or network. Additionally, the individuals they know are also a part of the network. Another dimension of social capital is relational social capital, which is defined by the strength of the relationship between two actors. For example, you may have a close friend that you have known your entire life and see weekly. The length of the relationship as well as the strength, in addition to the frequency of interaction, creates a strong tie between the two of you, or a high level of relational social capital. In comparison, you may have met another individual during the past year, and have seen him or her a few times at social functions. There is a lower level of relational social capital between the two of you when compared to that of your life-long friend. Cognitive social capital is shared language and codes. For example, two attorneys from different cities meet at a conference. Although they have never met before, so they do not share any structural or relational social capital, they begin to discuss the latest Supreme Court decisions. Because these two individuals share an understanding of legal language and codes, they are able to establish a relationship based upon these codes and language, thus creating cognitive social capital. The structural and relational dimensions of social capital have been found to influence the investments of VC firms. Cognitive social capital studies are few, so we include this dimension of social capital to better understand its influence on VC firm investments. We examine these dimensions to understand how they influence VC firms' investments in WLBs.

This paper is organized as follows. The next section briefly reviews the relevant literature on these topics and sets forth the hypotheses to be tested. The following section discusses the research design, including specific information on data gathering and preparation, the calculation of the variables, and the empirical model. The next section reports descriptive statistics, frequencies, and the findings of the study relative to the hypotheses. The fifth section discusses these results, and the final section provides concluding remarks.

LITERATURE REVIEW AND HYPOTHESES

Entrepreneurial firms have accounted for 65 percent to 90 percent of net new job creation in the United States during the past 15 years (Headd, 2010). One of the fastest growing groups of entrepreneurial firms is women-led businesses (Brush, De Bruin, & Welter, 2009). In 2008, women-led businesses (WLBs) had a $3 trillion annual impact on the U.S. economy and accounted for 16% of all U.S. jobs (Research, 2009). As a whole, these businesses "are the fastest-growing sector of new venture creation in the USA, representing nearly 40% of all firms" (Amatucci & Sohl, 2004). For all new firms, one of the key fundamental building blocks is money (Bates, Jackson, & Johnson, 2007). Research, however, has found that women-led businesses (WLBs) have lower levels of overall funding (Carter & Rosa, 1998; Watson, 2002) and receive significantly less VC funding than companies led by men (MLBs) (Brush, Carter, Gatewood, Greene, & Hart, 2004; Greene, Brush, Hart, & Saparito, 2001). Indeed, from 1997 to 2000, WLBs received *less than 6%* of the $185.5 billion in VC invested during this historic period of investment activity (Brush, Carter, Gatewood, Greene, & Hart, 2001). Studies point to multiple factors that explain this disparity. First, VC firms invest in high-growth companies with products targeted at growing markets (Gompers & Lerner, 2001) and WLBs tend to not be in these markets (Brush et al., 2004). Second, women's social networks tend to consist primarily of other women (Aldrich, 1989). As a result, these networks have a much smaller likelihood of including venture capitalists, because few of them are women (Brush et al., 2001). Finally, WLBs experience lower growth and profitability, due in part to limited access to funding and lower growth aspirations (Alsos, Isaksen, & Ljunggren, 2006). These factors may contribute to the perception that WLBs are more risky than MLBs (Cliff, 1998). In fact, Brophy (1997) states that women entrepreneurs "carry an extra burden of prejudgment" by potential investors (Brophy, 1997, p. 7). In other words, *VC firms may perceive* WLBs as possessing greater risk than MLBs. This perception of riskiness may influence VCs decisions to invest in WLBs. Even if a WLB is able to overcome these factors, Brush et al. (2004) state that an entrepreneur must have relevant network connections to even begin negotiating with venture capitalists.

These earlier studies, however, utilize data limited by timeframe (1997 to 2000) (Brush et al., 2001), location (Norway, Britain) (Alsos et al., 2006; Carter & Rosa, 1998) or type of funding (banking) (Carter, Shaw, Lam, & Wilson, 2007). Additionally, while such previous studies have advanced our understanding of how, why, and to what extent WLBs are funded, the predominant perspective has been from the WLB or demand-side. In this study, we take a more supply-side view, by considering VC investing in WLBs from the VC firm's perspective. We propose that networks and social capital factors specific to VC firms, rather than WLB firms, will influence the tendency to invest in WLBs. Our discussion of VC firms and their funding of WLBs follows.

Which Venture Capital Firms Invest in Women-Led Businesses?

Venture capital investments are important to high growth companies, with many VC backed companies going public or being acquired by larger firms (Busenitz, Arthurs, Hoskisson, & Johnson, 2003; Chang, 2004; Gulati & Higgins, 2003).

In fact, 20 out of 74, or 31%, of the companies that completed initial public offerings (IPOs) during the first half of 2010 were funded by VC firms (NASDAQ.com). These companies are innovative and create jobs, factors critical to economic growth. While firms receiving VC funding are a small percentage of new companies, they develop innovative products, create new jobs, and generate wealth for investors, entrepreneurs and employees (Arthurs & Busenitz, 2006; Chang, 2004).

Studies have found that entrepreneurs with a direct relationship with a VC firm or venture capitalist are more likely to receive VC funding than entrepreneurs without a direct tie to a VC firm (Hsu, 2007). This confirms earlier research (Fried & Hisrich, 1994) that VC firms seldom fund businesses that are not endorsed by a member of the VC network. In a similar vein, other studies have found that VC firms fund companies that are recommended by a trusted third party (Shane & Cable, 2002). In other words, the lack of a direct or indirect tie to a VC or VC firm is a significant handicap to entrepreneurs seeking VC funding.

From the VC perspective, VC firms use their social networks to source potential investment opportunities (Hochberg, Ljungqvist, & Lu, 2007). This use of such network references serves to decrease the risk associated with investing in start-up companies. New VC firms, however, do not have the network ties of more established VC firms and, thus, receive far less information regarding potential investment opportunities. Not surprisingly, new VC firms suffer from the same "liabilities of newness" (Stinchcombe, 1965) as any other new firm and have limited access to new deal flows.

Indeed, one study found that VC firms with fewer network ties (lower social capital) invest in riskier portfolio companies (Podolny, 2001). As discussed earlier, VC firms view WLBs as higher risk. The result of this view could result in new VC firms with limited network connections tending to invest in WLBs.

Does Investing in Women-Led Businesses Affect Future Venture Capital Firm Activity?

A VC firm's performance is solely a function of the success, or failure, of its portfolio companies. If the investments are successful, investors in the VC firm will receive a positive return on their investment, which, in turn, encourages investors to provide additional funding for the VC firm to invest in new portfolio companies. The performance of the WLB will therefore influence the VC' firm's performance and ability to raise future capital. How then, will investing in WLBs affect the VC firm's performance and subsequent investment practices?

It is possible that WLBs that receive VC funding are examined more thoroughly than MLBs receiving VC funding. The WLB may have endured more intensive due diligence on its product, management team, customers, etc. In other words, the WLB had to clear higher hurdles than the MLBs receiving VC funding. Other minority-owned business funded by VCs may have faced similar scrutiny. Research has found that minority-oriented VC firms investing in businesses owned by minorities (African Americans, Hispanic Americans and Asian Americans) had average internal rates of return (IRR) of 23.9 percent, compared with 20.2 percent for all U.S. VC firms (Bates & Bradford, 2003). We expect investing in WLBs may similarly affect VC firm performance.

Finally, as previously discussed, VCs invest in deals sourced from their networks. Once a VC firm invests in a WLB, a relationship is established between the VC firm and the WLB. In other words, the women executives in the WLB will now have a VC firm in their networks. These women may introduce or recommend members of their network to the VC firm. Since women tend to have a high percentage of women in their networks, the VC firm may receive more proposals from new WLBs and, if the initial investment was successful, increase their investments in new WLBs.

Hypotheses

Given the literature review, the study will test the following hypotheses:

1) Investment in WLBs by VC firms will be negatively associated with the VC firms' (a) relationships with other, well-connected VC firms, (b) relationships with other VC firms sharing the industry or investment stage focus, and (c) frequency and duration of co-investing with other, high-status VC firms.
2) VC firms' performance will be positively associated with investing in WLBs.
3) Future investment in WLBs by VC firms will be positively associated with previous investments in WLBs by these VC firms

RESEARCH DESIGN

The hypotheses developed in the previous section predict the influence of investing in WLBs on VC firm performance, as well as future investments in WLBs. The unit of analysis is the VC firm. The hypotheses are tested using panel data from 2000 through 2011. These data include repeated observations of variables for each VC firm. This dataset allows for reporting of fixed-effects regression estimates. Use of longitudinal data, as well as social network measures, create additional complexities.

Data Collection

The first step in data collection was to obtain every investment by a U.S.-based VC firm in a U.S.- based company (portfolio company) during the eleven-year period of 2000 through 2010 from the Thomson-Reuters VentureXpert database. These data include VC firm name, founding date, industry investing preference, investment stage preference, and zip code.

The data for investment transactions (rounds) include VC firm name(s), portfolio company name, and round date. Frequently, multiple VC firms co-invest with one another in a round. This co-investment is the basis for relationships among VC firms.

The data for portfolio companies include company name, founding date, industry, location, status (public, subsidiary, private, or defunct) and management team members' titles and first and last names. A portion of the names include prefixes of Mr., Ms., or Dr.

The dataset includes 2,500 VC firms, 18,900 portfolio companies, 92,500 individual management team members, and 90,000 investment rounds.

Gender Identification

The first step in gender identification was to identify each management team member's sex. This multi-phase process started with a review of those names with prefixes of Mr. or Ms. These data were sorted by first name and reviewed for appropriate gender identifier. All questionable prefixes, Mr. Barbara Jones, for example, were researched and corrected if necessary.

The next phase was to identify those individuals with Dr. or without a prefix. These data were also sorted by first name and those with obvious male (William or Robert, for example) or female (Deborah or Kathleen, for example) first names were assigned the appropriate prefix.

The final step was to assign gender prefixes to each individual with non-gender-specific names, such as Pat, Chris, Carol, Xin and Naghmeh. The multi-step process in identifying gender for these individuals included searching multiple databases, including Hoover's, BusinessWeek, Forbes, the Securities and Exchange Commission and LinkedIn. Also, many individuals were located on company websites. The use of name, company, location and title ensured the correct "Pat Jones" was identified in this process.

With the gender identification process completed, each portfolio company was coded as WLB if there was a female on the management team. This definition is consistent with extant WLB research (Brush, Carter, Gatewood, Greene & Hart, 2001; Brush, De Bruin, & Welter, 2009; for examples). All other portfolio companies were coded as MLB.

Performance Measures

Each portfolio company was identified in VentureXpert as public, subsidiary (acquired by or merged with another company), private, or defunct. Portfolio companies identified as public and subsidiary were included as exits in calculating firm performance.

Dependent Variables

We test our hypotheses using the ratio of investments in WLBs as the primary dependent variable (Brush, et al., 2004). Accordingly, we calculate the WLB Investment Ratio (WIR) for each VC firm i at time t as follows:

$$WIR_{it} = \text{No. of WLB Investments}_{it} / \text{Total No. of Investments}_{it} \qquad (1)$$

Consistent with extant research (Brush et al., 2001; Brush, Carter, Gatewood, Greene, & Hart, 2006) we identify a WLB as a portfolio company in which a woman is a member of the company's senior executive management team. Thus, to calculate the numerator for the dependent variable, we sum the number of portfolio companies with at least one woman as a member of the senior executive management team. This is a continuous variable with values between 0 and 1. We calculate this variable for time 0 (T0) and T1.

Our second dependent variable is VC firm performance. We calculate firm performance Perf for each VC firm i at time t as follows:

$$Perf_{it} = \text{No. of Portfolio Company Exits}_{it} / \text{Total No. of Investments}_{it} \qquad (2)$$

Consistent with extant research (Hochberg et al., 2007) we identify a portfolio company exit as the completion of an initial public offering (IPO) or merger with another company. This is a continuous variable with values between 0 and 1.

Independent Variables

Measures of VC Firm Social Capital
Lin (2001) defines social capital as "resources embedded in a social structure that are accessed and/or mobilized" (p. 29, italics added). In turn, Nahapiet and Ghoshal (1998: p. 243) state that social capital is "the sum of the actual and potential resources embedded within, available through, and derived from the network of relationships possessed by an individual or social unit." Thus, consistent with extant research, (Gulati & Higgins, 2003; Hochberg et al., 2007; Podolny, 2001), we identify a social network *tie* between two VC firms by their co-investment in the same portfolio company. These co-investments include both initial and subsequent rounds of financing.

Per prior research (Guler, 2007; Podolny, 2001), we will use a rolling three-year (36 month) window to define these co-investment ties. This shorter timeperiod reflects the velocity of the VC industry. More formally, in a matrix of VC co-investment ties for a given time period t, each element or dyad of the matrix equals 1 if VC firms i and j have co-investment in the prior 36 months and zero otherwise.

The social capital and network measures are based upon co-investing relationships, as described above. For example, both Accel Partners and Greylock Partners invested in Facebook in 2006. This co-investment results in a dyad of Accel and Greylock in 2006.

Crosstab matrices were created for each three-year period in 2000 through 2010. Each matrix was at 1,000 lines by 1,000 columns, each line and column representing a VC firm. These matrices were imported to UCINET VI and used to calculate degree centrality, closeness and structural holes measures. The dyad tables were used to calculate the relationship frequency and duration, as well as shared industry and investment stage focus. All social capital and network measures were calculated for rolling three-year periods.

The social capital established by such ties has at least three dimensions (Nahapiet & Ghoshal, 1998). The first is the *structural* aspect, which deals with whom you know and how you know them. The second is the *relational* aspect of social capital, which encompasses "those assets created and leveraged through relationships" (Nahapiet & Ghoshal, 1998). Finally, the *cognitive* aspect refers to the meanings, systems, and representations shared by the group or network. Thus, we will use the social network analysis program, UCINET VI, to calculate the social capital measures as described below.

Structural Social Capital

The concept of network centrality corresponds to the social structures that connect a given firm to other actors within an overall network. The three dimensions of network centrality explicated by Freeman (1979) are degree centrality, closeness, and structural holes (betweenness). We use all three measures of centrality to analyze the structural dimensions of social capital and the subsequent impact on WLB investments by VC firms.

Degree Centrality. Degree centrality indicates how "connected" a VC firm is to the other VC firms in the network. Specifically, it indicates that for a given VC firm the number of ties (i.e., degrees) to all otherVC firms is calculated as,

$$D_{it} = [d(n_i)]_t \qquad (3)$$

We define d(n$_i$) as the number of direct co-investment ties for VC firm i. As a result, if a VC firm has co-investments with every other VC firm in the network of 100, then its degree centrality measure will be 100. If, on the other hand, a VC firm has co-investments with only half of the VC firms in the network, then its degree centrality measure will be 50. This is a continuous variable. Per our hypotheses, we expect a VC firm's degree centrality to be related negatively to its WLB investment ratio.

Closeness. This measure indicates the "degrees of separation" between VC firms in a network. While there are numerous measures of closeness (Bavelas, 1950; Beauchamp, 1965; Moxley & Moxley, 1974; Rogers, 1974), we use the Sabidussi (1966) measure, which calculates closeness as follows:

$$C_{it} = [(g-1) / \textstyle\sum_j d(n_i, n_j)]_t \tag{4}$$

Again, g-1 is the total number of possible direct ties in the network, but in this case d(n$_i$, n$_j$) is the distance between VC firms i and j (Wasserman & Faust, 1994). The distance indicates the number of "moves" to connect VC firms i and j. A direct tie between VC firms i and j, for example, has a distance of 1, whereas an indirect tie established by a shared connection to a third VC firm has a distance of 2, and so on. This is a continuous variable.

Per our literature review and hypotheses, a high closeness score indicates how efficiently a VC firm can access information in the network through its links to other VC firms who are well connected. To be clear, a VC firm can have a high closeness score through a tie to another node with high degree centrality, even if the focal VC firm has few direct links in the network or low degree centrality. Again, we expect a VC firm's closeness to be related negatively to its WLB investment ratio.

Structural Holes. Burt's (1992) theory of structural holes highlights the importance of gaps in the structure of social networks where ties between actors fail to form. Such structural holes present opportunities for actors to "broker" connections across these gaps, but it also means these acts are less embedded (i.e., more autonomous) in the network. In fact, per our literature review, we contend that those VC firms that span structural holes have an advantage in terms of deal information flows.

We use a widely accepted indicator of structural holes to measure the degree of autonomy of a VC firm in the network (Burt, 1992). This measure follows from previous research (Podolny, 2001) and is calculated as follows:

$$A_{it} = [1 - \textstyle\sum_j (p_{ij} + \textstyle\sum_q p_{iq} p_{qj})^2]_t \tag{5}$$

where $i \neq j \neq q$

Here, p_{ij} is the proportion of VC firm i's total number of investment deals that are co-investments with VC firm j. In other words, p_{ij} is zero if VC firm i has no co-investments with VC firm j and is equal to 1 if all of i's investments are co-investments with j. In turn, the term $\Sigma q p_{iq} p_{qj}$ captures the indirect ties to firm j by the shared co-investment patterns with VC firm q. In particular, p_{iq} is the proportion of VC firm i's co-investments with VC firm q and p_{qj} is the proportion of VC firm q's co-investments with VC firm j. Thus, overall, the summed term in parentheses captures the direct $_{(p_{ii'})}$ and indirect ($\Sigma q p_{iq} p_{qi'}$) ties between VC firms i and j. More importantly, A_i ranges from 0 to 2 with lower values of A_i indicating the VC firm is more autonomous (i.e., spans many structural holes) and higher values indicating the VC firm is more deeply embedded in a network of redundant connections. This is a continuous variable.

Relational Social Capital
The preponderance of social capital research in business environments has focused on the relational dimension. This dimension of social capital can clearly be distinguished from the structural dimension because the former refers to the nature of the relationship between two actors (or nodes) in a dyad, whereas the latter refers to the relationships across multiple actors. Tie strength is frequently used as an independent variable in research on the relational dimension of social capital. The concept of strong and weak ties was explicated by Granovetter (1973), where tie strength was defined as a linear function of "a combination of the amount of time, the emotional intensity, the intimacy (mutual confiding) and the reciprocal services which characterize the tie" (p. 1361). However, since research on tie strength finds mixed results for single, rather than multiple, measures (Marsden, 2005; Marsden & Campbell, 1984), we use relationship duration and frequency as measures of relational social capital.

Relationship Duration. We calculate relationship duration in increments of six months from the first co-investment. That is, if a new VC firm invests with only one other VC firm and that relationship is a year old, the duration will be 2 (12 months divided by 6 months). In turn, we calculate the average tie duration for each VC firm by summing the individual duration measures and dividing that by the number of ties for that firm. Formally, the calculation is,

$$R_{it} = [\sum j(r_{ij}/6) / d(n_i)]_t \qquad (6)$$

where r_{ij} is the number of months since the first co-investment between VC firms i and j and $d(n_i)$ is the number of degrees (direct ties) for VC firm i. This is a continuous variable.

Relationship Frequency. We estimate relationship frequency by using a measure of multiplexity. In his study of VC firms, Podolny (2001) utilizes the number of shared deals to measure tie strength as a function of frequency of interaction. Thus, for this measure, each shared deal is defined as an investment in a *new* portfolio company, rather than an existing portfolio company. We then calculate an average multiplexity measure for each VC firm by summing the individual frequency measures for the VC firm and dividing that sum by the total number of ties for that firm. If a new VC firm co-invests with only one other VC firm, in three companies, this measure will be 3 (3 divided by 1). This measure is calculated as

$$M_i = [\sum s_{ij} / d(n_i)]_t \qquad (7)$$

where s_{ij} is the number of co-investments in *new* portfolio companies between VC firms i and j and $d(n_i)$ is the number of degrees (direct ties) for VC firm i. This is a continuous variable.

Cognitive Social Capital

Because empirical studies examining the cognitive aspect of social capital are scarce, if not nonexistent, we could not identify extant measures of cognitive social capital. Simsek, Lubatkin and Floyd (2003) propose a definition of firm-level cognitive embeddedness as "the degree of similarity among network actors...concerning their beliefs about types of issues perceived to be important, how such issues are conceptualized and, perhaps, alternative approaches for dealing with such issues" (Simsek, Lubatkin and Floyd, 2003, p.433). They do not, however, engage in empirical work on cognitive social capital.

It is common for VC firms to focus their investments in a specific industry (e.g., telecommunications or biotechnology) or investment stage. Thus, to capture the cognitive social capital of VCs we measure shared industry and investment stage foci. We calculate shared industry focus for each VC firm, where each co-investor focuses on the same specific industry, such as telecommunications or biotechnology.

Shared Industry Focus[i] If the focal VC firm co-invests with another VC firm that shares the same industry focus, we code it as a 1; if the industry focus is not the same, the coding is 0. In turn, we calculate the shared industry focus ratio by summing these and then dividing by the number of co-investors (ties) for that firm. Formally, the calculation is

$$IND_{it} = [\textstyle\sum_j u_{ij} / d(n_i)]_t \tag{8}$$

where u_{ij} is the number of shared industry focus co-investments between VC firms i and j and $d(n_i)$ is the number of degrees (direct ties) for VC firm i. This is a continuous variable.

Shared Investment Stage Focus[ii] Using this same approach, we calculate shared investment stage focus for each VC firm dyad, where investment-stage focus is defined as early, middle or late stage. The calculation is as follows:

$$INV_{it} = [\textstyle\sum_j v_{ij} / d(n_i)]_t \tag{9}$$

where v_{ij} is the number of shared investment-stage focus co-investments between VC firms i and j and $d(n_i)$ is the number of degrees (direct ties) for VC firm i. This is a continuous variable.

Control Variables

In addition to the social capital variables described above, the following control variables are defined for each VC firm. *VC Firm Age* is the number of months since the founding date of the firm. *VC Firm Location* is the state in which the firm's primary office is located. Dummy variables were used for Massachusetts, New York, California, Texas and Illinois. These five states were selected because they are the top 5 states where VCs make investments and they make up 62.2% of all VC investments. We utilized dummy variables for each year, 2001 through 2010.

Model Specification

To test our model, we estimate a system of two simultaneous equations for two reasons. First, our data violate the independence assumption of normal regression models, as the social capital measures are non-independent based on the method of calculation. As an example, two of the structural social capital measures—degree centrality and closeness—share, respectively, the same information in the numerator and denominator. Second, there is the issue of endogeneity introduced by the simultaneity of the dependent variable and the VC firm performance variable as well as an omitted variable bias. As a result, we estimate the following system of equations:

$$WIR_{it} = \beta X_{it} + Perf_{it} + \varepsilon_{it} \tag{10}$$

$$Perf_{it} = \beta X_{it} + {}_{WIR_{it}} + \varepsilon_{it} \tag{11}$$

We estimate this system of equations via three-stage least squares (3SLS) estimation. By combining instrumented variable or two-stage least squares (2SLS) estimation with seemingly unrelated regression (SUR), three-stage least squares can handle many of the expected irregularities in our data and model specifications while relaxing many of the MLE assumptions and providing a full set of diagnostic tools and procedures.

RESULTS

Descriptive statistics are reported in Table 1. One surprising result is that the average ratio of investing in WLBs is 41%. This differs from earlier reported data where WLBs receive only 6% of VC funding. This difference is due to two factors: first, our measure is the investment in WLBs, not the dollar amount invested. Further, our data are for all VC investments during the 11 year period. Earlier studies examined only those transactions where funding data were available for a 2 year period. We believe the extensive data utilized in this study support our analysis and conclusions and reflect the investments in WLBs.

Table 1. Descriptive Statistics

	Minimum	Maximum	Mean	Std. Deviation
WLB Ratio	.00	1.00	.4131	.33312
WLB Ratio T1	.00	1.00	.4131	.33312
Success Ratio	.00	1.00	.1597	.25950
Closeness	50.037090	55.639099	50.32141026	.447813867
Degree	2	255	16.20	22.069

Table 1. (Continued)

	Minimum	Maximum	Mean	Std. Deviation
Structural Holes	.5621188	1.9966847	1.135608892	.3274860557
Frequency	.06	4.27	1.1286	.60667
Duration	.00	139.05	27.5291	22.21675
Shared Industry Focus Ratio	.00	4.05	.8570	.65937
Shared Investment Focus Ratio	.00	4.05	.8585	.65777
MA	0	1	.09	.288
CA	0	1	.27	.444
NY	0	1	.16	.367
TX	0	1	.05	.221
IL	0	1	.05	.217
Age	0	99	10.12	9.247

Table 2 shows the results of our testing of our first hypothesis – the impact of social capital on investing in WLBs. As noted in Model 1, our base model, the significant control variables are age, the states of Massachusetts and California, as well as the dummy variables for years 2002, 2004, 2005, and 2008.

Table 2. Dependent Variable WLB Investment Ratio

	Model 1		Model 2		Model 3		Model 4	
(Constant)	.349	***	-1.794		.435	***	.432	***
2001	.003		-.080	***	-.093	***	-.073	***
2002	.034	**	-.039	*	-.042	*	-.036	
2003	.019		-.017		-.034	*	-.012	
2004	.039	**	-.023		-.045	**	-.023	
2005	.033	**	-.047	**	-.055	***	-.047	**
2006	.006		-.031		-.038	*	-.023	
2007	.025		-.038		-.053	**	-.030	
2008	.036	**	-.027		-.034		-.026	
2009	.012		-.035		-.041	**	-.030	
2010	.014		-.013		-.037	*	-.017	
MA	.035	***	.025		.019		.021	
CA	.042	***	.021		.023		.019	
NY	.010		.018		.024		.025	
TX	-.022		-.033	**	-.034	**	-.035	**
IL	.013		.010		.008		.014	
Age	.031	***	.012		.004		.011	
Closeness			-.573					

	Model 1		Model 2		Model 3		Model 4	
Degree			.610					
Structural Holes			-.074	***				
Frequency					.056	***		
Duration					.107	***		
Shared Industry Focus							.039	
Shared Investment Stage Focus							.080	
R-Squared	0.09		0.13		0.14		0.16	
F-Statistic	7.764		7.525		8.561		9.896	
N	13638		13638		13638		13638	

*significant at .01, ** significant at .005, *** significant <.001.

In Model 2 we include the measures of structural social capital. Interestingly, both closeness and structural holes had the negative impact we hypothesized, but only the structural holes variable was significant. The significance of age and Massachusetts and California lost significance. Texas, however, was significant and negative. Hypothesis 1 is partially supported for structural social capital.

In Model 3, we introduce the relational social capital measures. Both frequency and duration of the relationships among VC firms were significant, but positive. Hypothesis 1 is not supported for relational social capital.

In Model 4, our measures of cognitive social capital are not significant, thus not supporting hypothesis 1 for cognitive social capital.

Table 3. Dependent Variable Success Ratio

	Model 1		Model 2	
(Constant)	.155	***	.128	***
2001	.156	***	.156	***
2002	.097	***	.093	***
2003	.060	***	.058	***
2004	.028	*	.024	
2005	-.031	**	-.034	***
2006	-.063	***	-.064	***
2007	-.087	***	-.090	***
2008	-.110	***	-.113	***
2009	-.058	***	-.059	***
2010	-.042	***	-.044	***
MA	-.007		-.011	
CA	.005		.001	
NY	.041	***	.040	***
TX	-.021	*	-.019	

Table 3. (Continued)

	Model 1		Model 2	
IL	-.005		-.006	
Age	.048	***	.045	***
WLB Investment Ratio			.101	***
R-Squared	0.173		0.183	
F-Statistic	178.398		179.784	
N	13638		13638	

*significant at .01, ** significant at .005, *** significant <.001.

    Table 3 includes the results of our testing of hypothesis 2, that investing in WLBs will have a positive influence on VC firm performance. The dependent variable is the VC firm's success ratio. Model 1 is our base model and Model 2 includes the independent variable of WLB investment ratio. The effect of WLB investment ratio on VC firm success is positive and significant, supporting hypothesis 2.

    Table 4 shows the results of our testing of hypothesis 3. The dependent variable is the subsequent investment in WLBs. Again, Model 1 is our base model and Model 2 included the earlier investment in WLBs. The effect of the WLB investment ratio is positive and significant, supporting hypothesis 3.

Table 4. Dependent Variable Subsequent Investment in WLBs

	Model 1		Model 2	
(Constant)	.349	***	.325	***
2001	.003		-.016	
2002	.034	**	.023	
2003	.019		.012	
2004	.039	**	.035	**
2005	.033	**	.037	**
2006	.006		.013	
2007	.025		.036	**
2008	.036	**	.049	***
2009	.012		.019	
2010	.014		.020	
MA	.035	***	.036	***
CA	.042	***	.041	***
NY	.010		.005	
TX	-.022		-.019	
IL	.013		.014	

	Model 1		Model 2	
Age	.031	***	.025	**
Investment in WLBs at T0			.121	*
R-Squared	.009			
F-Statistic	7.764			
N	13638		13638	

*significant at .01, ** significant at .005, *** significant <.001.

DISCUSSION

As discussed above, our findings show partial support for our first hypothesis regarding the influence of social capital on a VC firm's investments in WLBs. Interestingly, structural social capital, specifically structural holes, has the hypothesized negative effect on investing in WLBs. This is similar to the earlier research finding that VC firms spanning more structural holes invested in "safer" investments. Another aspect of our findings is that the three measures of structural social capital have different effects on investing in WLBs. This supports the belief that the different dimensions of structural social capital result in different outcomes.

Our findings did not support our thesis that relational social capital had a negative influence on the ratio of investments in WLBs. Unexpectedly, both frequency and duration had significant and positive results. One interpretation of these results is that VC firms that co-invest frequently with the same firms tend to invest more in WLBs because they are able to share the risk of the investment with other VC firms.

Our cognitive social capital measures were not significant. This may be because our measure doesn't capture cognitive social capital. As discussed earlier, extant research has not identified cognitive social capital measures, so our measures were exploratory. This does not mean that cognitive social capital is not a valid construct, but that the ability to measure it remains elusive.

Finally, overall, our findings support the belief that there are multiple dimensions of social capital and these dimensions may have different, even conflicting, effects on outcomes. It would be interesting to examine the interaction of these measures to gain a greater understanding of social capital's influence on VC firm investment decisions.

Our second hypotheses, that investing in WLBs results in improved VC firm performance was supported. This may be the result of more vigorous due diligence on WLBs compared with MLBs or the influence of a heterogeneous management team.

Finally, our third hypothesis that VC firm initial investment in WLBs would lead to subsequent investments in WLBs was supported. Additionally, we tested the influence of the VC firm success measure on the future tendency to invest in WLBs and the results were also positive and significant.

CONCLUSION

This study set out to explore the effects of VC firm social capital on investing in WLBs. Our approach to the question of VC funding of WLBs was different from extant research in that we viewed the question from the perspective of the VC firm, rather than the WLB. Our analysis indicates that VC firms' social capital influences their investments in WLBs, but in different and sometimes conflicting ways. The investment in WLBs does have a positive influence on VC firms' results, measured as the public offering or acquisition of portfolio companies in which the VC firm has invested.

Further analysis is certainly called for. An examination of the effect of the interaction of the various dimensions of social capital on WLB investment could be a first step. One also wonders how these results would be affected if the definition of a WLB is limited to firms with women founders. A number of the women executives in these portfolio companies are in administrative roles, such as finance or human resources. This finer grained examination may improve our understanding of the factors affecting the funding of WLBs.

Descriptive Statistics

	N	Minimum	Maximum	Mean	Std. Deviation
Sum of Females	18913	.0	28.0	.618	1.1336
Max of Round Number	18913	1	24	3.20	2.617
Founding Date	15754	1/01/1813	12/01/2010	12/11/1994	6150
					21:09:38.089
Valid N (listwise)	15754				

Figure 1. Portfolio Company Descriptive Statistics.

Status

		Frequency	Percent	Valid Percent	Cumulative Percent
Valid	Defunct	697	3.7	3.7	3.7
	Private	15080	79.7	79.7	83.4
	Public	1293	6.8	6.8	90.3
	Registration	2	.0	.0	90.3
	Status Unknown	1	.0	.0	90.3
	Subsidiary	1824	9.6	9.6	99.9
	Withdrew Registration	16	.1	.1	100.0
	Total	18913	100.0	100.0	

Figure 2. Portfolio Company Status Statistics.

Industry Group

		Frequency	Percent	Valid Percent	Cumulative Percent
Valid	Biotechnology	1031	5.5	5.5	5.5
	Communications and Media	2147	11.4	11.4	16.8
	Computer Related	6541	34.6	34.6	51.4
	Medical/Health/Life Science	2105	11.1	11.1	62.5
	Non-High-Technology	6059	32.0	32.0	94.6
	Semiconductors/Other Elect	1030	5.4	5.4	100.0
	Total	18913	100.0	100.0	

Figure 3. Portfolio Company Industry Statistics.

Number of Rounds

		Frequency	Percent	Valid Percent	Cumulative Percent
Valid	1	6357	33.6	33.6	33.6
	2	3626	19.2	19.2	52.8
	3	2591	13.7	13.7	66.5
	4	1855	9.8	9.8	76.3

		Frequency	Percent	Valid Percent	Cumulative Percent
	5	1342	7.1	7.1	83.4
	6	1079	5.7	5.7	89.1
	7	665	3.5	3.5	92.6
	8	491	2.6	2.6	95.2
	9	314	1.7	1.7	96.9
	10	203	1.1	1.1	97.9
	11	138	.7	.7	98.7
	12	79	.4	.4	99.1
	13	61	.3	.3	99.4
	14	48	.3	.3	99.7
	15	22	.1	.1	99.8
	16	14	.1	.1	99.9
	17	12	.1	.1	99.9
	18	4	.0	.0	99.9
	20	3	.0	.0	100.0
	21	3	.0	.0	100.0
	22	2	.0	.0	100.0
	23	3	.0	.0	100.0
	24	1	.0	.0	100.0
	Total	18913	100.0	100.0	

Figure 4. Frequency of Rounds.

Number of Female Managers

		Frequency	Percent	Valid Percent	Cumulative Percent
Valid.	0	12123	64.1	64.1	64.1
	1.0	4053	21.4	21.4	85.5
	2.0	1641	8.7	8.7	94.2
	3.0	619	3.3	3.3	97.5
	4.0	236	1.2	1.2	98.7
	5.0	118	.6	.6	99.3
	6.0	47	.2	.2	99.6
	7.0	29	.2	.2	99.8
	8.0	19	.1	.1	99.9
	9.0	6	.0	.0	99.9
	10.0	11	.1	.1	99.9
	11.0	5	.0	.0	100.0
	13.0	2	.0	.0	100.0

	Frequency	Percent	Valid Percent	Cumulative Percent
14.0	1	.0	.0	100.0
17.0	1	.0	.0	100.0
22.0	1	.0	.0	100.0
28.0	1	.0	.0	100.0
Total	18913	100.0	100.0	

Figure 5. Frequency of Female Managers.

Descriptive Statistics

	N	Minimum	Maximum	Mean	Std. Deviation
WLB Company Ratio	2414	.000	1.000	.38894	.293790
WLB Investments Ratio	2414	.000	1.000	.39901	.303335
Success Ratio	2414	.000	1.000	.18255	.241072
Structural Holes Measure	2005	.620	1.999	1.14113	.334733
Number of ties	2005	2.0	417.0	24.635	38.1175
California=1	2414	0	1	.25	.433
Texas=1	2414	0	1	.06	.231
New York State=1	2414	0	1	.16	.371
Mass=1	2414	0	1	.08	.275
Illinois=1.	2414	0	1	.05	.211
Firm age in years	2312	1	100	14.26	9.328
Valid N (listwise)	1919				

Figure 6. VC Firm Statistics.

	Frequency	Percent	Valid Percent	Cumulative Percent
	843	6.7	6.7	6.7
Acquisition	705	5.6	5.6	12.3
Balanced	1090	8.7	8.7	21.0
Control-block Purchases	24	.2	.2	21.2
Distressed Debt	77	.6	.6	21.9
Early Stage	3781	30.2	30.2	52.0
Expansion	841	6.7	6.7	58.7
First Stage Financing	363	2.9	2.9	61.6
Fund of Funds	26	.2	.2	61.8

Fund of Funds of Second	4	.0	.0	61.9
Generalist PE	255	2.0	2.0	63.9
Industry Rollups	17	.1	.1	64.0
Joint Ventures	6	.0	.0	64.1
Later Stage	539	4.3	4.3	68.4
Leveraged Buyout	1558	12.4	12.4	80.8
Management Buyouts	163	1.3	1.3	82.1
Mezzanine	304	2.4	2.4	84.5
Open Market	10	.1	.1	84.6
Other	57	.5	.5	85.1
Private Placement	12	.1	.1	85.2
Public Companies	23	.2	.2	85.3
Recapitalizations	202	1.6	1.6	87.0
Research and Development	57	.5	.5	87.4
Second Stage Financing	165	1.3	1.3	88.7
Seed	801	6.4	6.4	95.1
Special Situation	56	.4	.4	95.6
Start-up Financing	184	1.5	1.5	97.0
Startup	306	2.4	2.4	99.5
Turnaround	66	.5	.5	100.0
Total	12535	100.0	100.0	

Figure 7. VC Firm Investment Stages.

GLOSSARY

Industry Stage – The stage in the life-cycle of a portfolio company. VC firms often prefer to invest in particular industry stages. For a listing of the industry stage classifications used in this paper, see Figure 7.

Social Capital – The benefit found in the relationship between two or more actors. For example, knowing the President of a local bank could provide benefits to an individual. There are three dimensions of social capital.

Cognitive Social Capital – The shared codes, terms or language of a group. For example, members of the military have shared language and terms, such as "deployment" or "TDY" that carry unique meanings in the military environment.

Relational Social Capital – The strength of the relationship between two or more actors. For example, immediate family members may have strong relational social capital. Neighbors in a large city might have weak social capital. Relational social capital is measured by frequency of interaction, duration of relationship and depth of confiding.

Structural Social Capital – The existence of a relationship between two or more actors. Frequently described as a "tie". A tie exists between two actors if they know each other. Structural social capital also includes the ties among a group of actors.

REFERENCES

Aldrich, H. 1989. Networking Among Women Entrepreneurs. In O. Hagan & C. Rivchun & D. L. Sexton (Eds.), *Women-Owned Businesses*: 103-132. New York, NY: Praeger.

Alsos, G. A., Isaksen, E. J., & Ljunggren, E. 2006. New Venture Financing and Subsequent Business Growth in Men- and Women-Led Businesses. *Entrepreneurship: Theory & Practice*, 30(5): 667-686.

Amatucci, F. & Sohl, J. 2004. Women Entrepreneurs Securing Business Angel Financing: Tales from the Field. *Venture Capital*, 6(2/3): 181-196.

Arthurs, J. D. & Busenitz, L. W. 2006. Dynamic Capabilities and Venture Performance: The Effects of Venture Capitalists. *Journal of Business Venturing*, 21(2): 195-215.

Bates, T. & Bradford, W. 2003. Minorities and Venture Capital: A New Wave in American Business: Kauffman Foundation.

Bates, T., Jackson, W. E. I., & Johnson, J. H. J. 2007. Introduction to the special issue on advancing research on minority entrepreneurship. *Annals of the American Academy of Political Science and Social Science*, 613: 10-17.

Brophy, D. J. 1997. Financing the Growth of Entrepreneurial Firms. In D. L. Sexton & R. W. Smilor (Eds.), *Entrepreneurship 2000*: 5-28. Chicago, Ill: Upstart Publishing Company.

Brush, C., Carter, N., Gatewood, E., Greene, P., & Hart, M. 2001. An Investigation of Women-Led Firms and Venture Capital Investment: U.S. Small Business Administration, Office of Advocacy, National Women's Business Council.

Brush, C., Carter, N., Gatewood, E., Greene, P., & Hart, M. 2004. Gatekeepers of Venture Growth: A Diana Report on the Role and Participation of

Women in the Venture Capital Industry. Kansas City, MO: Kauffman Foundation.

Brush, C., De Bruin, A., & Welter, F. 2009. A Gender-Aware Framework for Women's Entrepreneurship. *International Journal of Gender and Entrepreneurship*, 1(1): 8-24.

Busenitz, L. W., Arthurs, J. D., Hoskisson, R. E., & Johnson, R. A. 2003. Venture capitalists and information asymmetries in the pricing of IPO securities. *Academy of Management Proceedings*: E1-E6.

Carter, S. & Rosa, P. 1998. The financing of male- and female-owned businesses. *Entrepreneurship & Regional Development*, 10(3): 225-241.

Carter, S., Shaw, E., Lam, W., & Wilson, F. 2007. Gender, Entrepreneurship, and Bank Lending: The Criteria and Processes Used by Bank Loan Officers in Assessing Applications. *Entrepreneurship: Theory & Practice*, 31(3): 427-444.

Chang, S. J. 2004. Venture capital financing, strategic alliances, and the initial public offerings of Internet startups. *Journal of Business Venturing*, 19(5): 721-741.

Cliff, J. E. 1998. Does one size fit all? exploring the relationship between attitudes towards growth, gender, and business size. *Journal of Business Venturing*, 13(6): 523-542.

Fried, V. H. & Hisrich, R. D. 1994. Toward a Model of Venture Capital Investment Decision Making. *Financial Management*, 23: 28-37.

Gompers, P. & Lerner, J. 2001. The Venture Capital Revolution. *Journal of Economic Perspectives*, 15(2): 145-168.

Greene, P. G., Brush, C. G., Hart, M. M., & Saparito, P. 2001. Patterns of venture capital funding: is gender a factor? *Venture Capital: An International Journal of Entrepreneurial Finance*, 3(1): 63-83.

Gulati, R. & Higgins, M. C. 2003. Which Ties Matter When? The Contingent Effects Of Interorganizational Partnerships On IPO Success. *Strategic Management Journal*, 24(2): 127 - 144.

Headd, B. 2010. An Analysis of Small Business and Jobs: Small Business Administration, Office of Advocacy.

Hochberg, Y. V., Ljungqvist, A., & Lu, Y. 2007. Whom You Know Matters: Venture Capital Networks and Investment Performance. *Journal of Finance*, 62(1): 251.

Hsu, D. H. 2007. Experienced Entrepreneurial Founders, Organizational Capital, and Venture Capital Funding. *Research Policy*, 36: 722-741.

Podolny, J. M. 2001. Networks as Pipes and Prisms of the Market. *American Journal of Sociology*, 107(1): 33-60.

Research, C. f. W. s. B. 2009. The Economic Impact of Women-Owned Businesses in the United States: 1 - 12 Center for Women's Business Research.

Shane, S. & Cable, D. 2002. Network Ties, Reputation, and the Financing of New Ventures. *Management Science*, 48(Issue 3): 364-381.

Stinchcombe, A. L. 1965. Social Structure and Organizations. In J. G. March (Ed.), *Handbook of Organizations*. Chicago: Rand McNally & Company.

Watson, J. 2002. Comparing the Performance of Male- and Female-Controlled Businesses: Relating Outputs to Inputs. *Entrepreneurship: Theory & Practice*, 26(3): 91-100.

End Notes

[i] VC firms tend to invest in specific industries, such as hardware, software, social media, etc. We include a list of the industry classifications used in this study in Figure 3.

[ii] Portfolio companies are classified by their stage of development. VC firms may focus on a specific stage of development, such as early stage, later development, etc. These stages reflect the progress a portfolio company has made since founding. We include a list of these stages in Figure 7.

In: Capital Access   ISBN: 978-1-62948-197-5
Editors: H. Drexler and G. Maines   © 2013 Nova Science Publishers, Inc.

Chapter 3

THE VIABILITY OF THE MINORITY-ORIENTED VENTURE CAPITAL INDUSTRY: IMPLICATIONS OF DIVERSIFYING INVESTMENT STRATEGIES[*]

William E. Jackson III and Timothy Bates

EXECUTIVE SUMMARY

Since the 1990s, minority-oriented equity-capital funds, popularly known as venture capital (VC) funds, have substantially increased the size and scope of their small-business equity investments, particularly in firms owned by African Americans and Hispanics. Flush with capital raised from institutional investors in the 1990s, these venture-capital funds collectively have invested increasingly in new-economy high-tech lines of business in recent years. As high-tech investing has grown in popularity, the minority-oriented funds' investment practices have begun to resemble those of their mainstream (not minority oriented) VC-industry counterparts. This changing emphasis, along with a growing propensity to invest in white-owned firms, has coincided with substantial declines in the average returns generated by the minority-oriented VC funds in recent years. Why would these funds in the 21st century

---

[*] This report, released May 2013, was written by William E. Jackson, University of Alabama and Timothy Bates, Wayne State University, under a contract with the Small Business Administration, Office of Advocacy.

increasingly invest outside of their traditional minority-market niche? What are the ramifications of these investment trends for black- and Hispanic-owned ventures seeking venture capital financing? Why, finally, have the realized returns earned by the minority-oriented VC funds declined in the 21st century? Answers to these and closely related questions are developed and explained in this report.

Past studies have consistently demonstrated that minority-owned business enterprises (MBEs), particularly those owned by African Americans and Hispanics, have less access to debt and equity capital than similarly situated white-owned firms. When MBEs experience restricted access to capital markets, this market segment is being underserved and attractive returns may be available to funds choosing to specialize in financing this minority-business client group. This situation, which we call the "underserved market" hypothesis, indeed, constitutes the traditional rationale for the existence of minority-oriented VC funds.

We proceed by investigating the financial returns minority-oriented VC funds have earned on their realized equity investments initiated during the 1989 through 2004 time period. In cooperation with the National Association of Investment Companies (NAIC) and the E.M. Kauffman Foundation, extensive data describing the characteristics and strategies of VC funds serving the MBE market segment, along with detailed information on the equity investments in small businesses these funds have initiated since 1989, are now available to researchers. These data have been analyzed in this study. Our analysis sought to explain the financial returns generated by the investments of minority-oriented VC funds, and this was accomplished by analyzing detailed annual cash flow information through year end 2006 for each individual investment.

To understand the investment choices made by minority VC funds, it is necessary to situate those choices in the context of the strategies these funds employ to manage successfully the considerable risks inherent in making equity investments in their portfolio firms. Widespread syndication is symptomatic of the extensive networking that typifies the minority-oriented venture-capital funds. Through membership in the NAIC and their frequent cooperation in developing syndicated business investments, these funds are able to finance large deals while enhancing diversification of their investment portfolios. Second, nearly all of the VC fund general partners (GPs) actively participate in the affairs of their portfolio companies – sitting on boards of directors and involving the GPs in such managerial functions as assistance with hiring, engaging in active day-by-day managerial decision making, and participating in long-run planning. Finally, the minority-oriented VC funds, instead of focusing narrowly on a single industry, often rely on a diverse industry mix of portfolio companies; they are typically more broadly diversified than the mainstream venture-capital industry.

We have identified, using generalized least squares random effects regression analysis techniques, the fund traits and strategies that predict high investment returns on the realized equity investments of the minority-focused VC funds. We conducted these tests to determine the fund characteristics and strategies that are correlated with internal rates of return (IRR) values of individual VC investments in firms. Our analysis introduced control variables expected to impact investment returns, including equity investment dollar amounts, investment timing, portfolio company industry of operation, and VC fund vintage.

What profiles and strategies typify the more successful, as opposed to the less successful minority VC funds? Higher IRR values are associated with 1) investing in MBEs, 2) activism in assisting portfolio companies on the part of the VC fund general partners, and 3) a larger number of VC investments per fund general partner. It is noteworthy that all of these traits linked to higher returns on VC investments represent investing strategies employed at the discretion of the individual VC funds. Lower IRR values are associated with 1) making investments in white-owned firms, 2) being an older VC fund, 3) participating in syndicated investments, and 4) top of-the-cycle investing (making investments initially funded in either 1999 or 2000). Investing in high-tech companies, finally, has not been a productive strategy for minority-oriented VC funds seeking to generate high financial returns on their equity investments.

These findings validate the underserved minority market hypothesis: investing in MBEs, other factors being the same, generates higher returns for the minority VC funds than investments in nonminority-owned ventures. In English, this means that investments of the same dollar amount, initiated in the same time period, by minority-oriented VC funds using identical strategies regarding such factors as syndication, investment by industry, GP activism with portfolio companies, and the like, produced higher IRR values if the portfolio company was minority owned and lower values if the company was white owned.

Utilizing our regression analysis results and related findings, we attribute the generally declining financial returns typifying the minority-oriented VC funds in recent years to five factors, three of which reflect the tendency of these funds to emulate mainstream VC industry investing practices. First, cooperation among funds in the form of syndicated investing has declined, a trend mirroring mainstream investing practices. We attribute declining returns to the fact that minority VC funds are increasingly keeping their most promising investments entirely for themselves, while syndicating the less promising deals in order to spread the risk of a poor ultimate outcome for these deals. Second, the increasing frequency of investments in white-owned portfolio companies— rather than MBEs – has clearly depressed realized investment returns. Major institutional investors tend to prefer to provide investment capital to minority-oriented VC funds that emulate mainstream VC industry investing practices. Our analysis suggests that public pension funds and funds of funds – the two dominant sources of institutional investor funding for minority VC funds— collectively prefer to provide investment capital to minority VC funds investing in portfolio firms having racially diverse owners – white-owned as well as minority-owned ventures. Investing in hi-tech companies, third, is another factor tending to lower returns on realized equity investments in portfolio companies.

Investments initially funded in the years 1999 or 2000 by minority-oriented funds — investing at the very top of the VC industry's boom/bust cycle – were the fourth cause of low realized returns on VC investments; in comparison, investments initiated before or after 1999 and 2000 were much more successful. Investing heavily at the top of a boom/bust cycle, while certainly a negative, is most likely a transitory phenomenon rather than a strategic choice likely to indicate enduring poor returns on the equity investments made by the minority-oriented VC funds. Fund vintage, finally, shaped investing returns, a finding that suggests, on balance, a brighter future for the minority-oriented VC fund sector. The older funds were the ones most often producing low returns on realized equity investments, holding other factors constant, while the newer-generation funds – those most directly shaping the future trajectory – were the better performers. These newer VC funds are typically run by GPs possessing work experience in investment banking prior to launching their venture capital funds, while GPs of older funds rarely possessed such mainstream work experience. Our findings suggest that having prior work experience in investment banking conveyed investing advantages.

The question "why would these VC funds in the 21st century increasingly invest outside of their traditional minority market niche?" is closely linked to the investing preferences of the institutional investors that provide the funding for the venture capital industry. Major institutional investors like pension funds seek high financial returns when they invest in VC funds. When they contemplate investing into minority-oriented VC funds, they seek to cherry-pick the winners, investing only in the subset of minority funds poised to generate above-average returns for their institutional investors. In the process of picking and choosing those funds potentially offering the highest investment returns, the institutional investors effectively shape the trajectory of the minority VC industry subsector. The winners—flush with funding —rapidly achieve growing prominence in the MBE equity investing realm; the losers— smaller in resources available for investing—lose relative position within the minority VC fund universe.

Our findings and those of other researchers indicate that the dominant institutional investors providing funding to the minority-oriented VC funds have systematically tended to invest in the less profitable VC funds, including those investing most actively in hi-tech and white-owned portfolio companies. Importantly, however, the investing practices of these institutional capital sources are self-correcting over time precisely because their funding decisions are driven largely by their search for above-average returns. We therefore see this institutional investor set of preferences as a short-term phenomenon, with future funding flowing increasingly to the minority-oriented VC funds pursuing the equity investing strategies most clearly identified with generating high returns on their VC investments. Investing in minority-owned business ventures will remain dominant because they offer higher returns, on balance, than investments in firms owned by nonminority whites.

I. OVERVIEW AND BACKGROUND

A. Overview of the Minority-Oriented Venture Capital Industry

Since the 1990s, minority-oriented equity-capital funds, popularly known as venture capital (VC) funds, have substantially increased the size and scope of their small business equity investments, particularly in firms owned by African Americans and Hispanics (Bates and Bradford, 2008a). Flush with capital raised from institutional investors in the mid- to-late 1990s, these venture capital funds collectively have invested heavily in new-economy high-tech lines of business in recent years. As high-tech investing has grown in popularity, the minority-oriented funds' investment practices increasingly resemble those of their mainstream VC-industry counterparts. This changing emphasis, along with a growing propensity to invest in white nonminority-owned firms, has coincided with substantial declines in the average returns generated by equity investments of minority-oriented funds in recent years.

Why would these minority-oriented VC funds in the 21st century increasingly invest outside of their traditional minority market niche? Why would funds choose to focus increasingly upon financing high-tech firms, emulating the investment patterns of mainstream equity capital funds, if indeed their traditional minority-business-enterprise (MBE) clientele provided an underserved market segment offering attractive returns to equity capital funds targeting this client group (Bates and Bradford, 2008a)? What are the ramifications of these investment trends for black- and Hispanic-owned ventures seeking venture capital financing? Why, finally, have the realized returns earned by the minority-oriented VC funds declined in the 21st century? Has their increased orientation toward the investing practices of mainstream VC funds reduced returns for the minority-oriented VC funds? If so, is it the growth of investing in nonminority-owned business ventures, the increase in high-tech investing, or other factors that have reduced the returns generated by realized equity investments of the minority-oriented VC funds? Investing trends shaped by the preferences of large institutional investors possibly encourage the growth of minority-oriented equity-capital-investing funds that generate below-average returns and invest less equity capital in minority-owned small businesses. Perhaps it is some combination of these factors. Answers to these questions are derived and explained in this report.

Scholarly studies have consistently demonstrated that minority-owned business enterprises (MBEs), particularly those owned by African Americans and Hispanics, have less access to debt and equity capital than similarly situated white-owned firms (see, for example, Cavalluzzo and Wolken, 2005; Bates and Bradford, 1992; Blanchflower, et al., 2003). When MBEs experience restricted access to capital markets, this market segment is being underserved and attractive returns may be available to funds choosing to specialize in financing this minority-business client group. This reasoning is the crux of the "underserved market" hypothesis, and available evidence is consistent with this hypothesis (Bates and Bradford, 2008a; Bates and Bradford, 2003)[1]. The underserved market hypothesis, indeed, constitutes the traditional rationale for the existence of minority-oriented equity-investing venture capital funds.

Venture capital funds specializing in making equity investments in minority-owned business enterprises have become important sources of equity capital for MBEs. Their growth has been driven primarily by the willingness of major institutional investors – particularly public pension funds – to commit financial capital to this traditionally neglected niche. In the process, the investment practices of VC funds targeting equity investments in MBEs have been shaped by the preferences of institutional investors (Bates and Bradford, 2009). Institutional investors have directed their investments increasingly toward minority-oriented VC funds investing in "new-economy" lines of business. While high-tech investing has grown, high returns have flowed more often to the funds investing most actively in "old-economy" fields (Bates and Bradford, 2008b).

Does diversifying outside the underserved minority market niche increase or decrease the availability of management support services and/or the amount of equity capital that minority-oriented VC funds provide when investing in minority-owned small businesses? The issues we explore are whether diversification into nonminority investments by minority-oriented VC funds has helped or hurt the access of minority-owned small businesses to equity capital and related management assistance services. We recognize that equity capital markets are not "zero-sumgames" and that investing a portion of VC-fund equity capital in nonminority owned firms does not necessarily equate to investing less equity capital in minority-owned small businesses. If, for example, diversification into nonminority investing allows minority-oriented VC funds to grow relatively more rapidly, then diversification may actually increase the absolute size of the potential pool of investable funds available to VC funds to invest in MBEs. Fortunately, our extensive data set describing minority-oriented VC funds and their investments developed in previous studies provides insights into these issues.

B. Minority Business Enterprise Access to Venture Capital: The Relevance of Capital Constraints

Minority-oriented venture-capital funds have been able to attract capital from such major institutional investors as pension funds because these investors anticipate that yields forthcoming from their VC fund investments will be competitive with the yields available from alternative investments. Of course, venture capital generally is regarded as substantially riskier and less liquid than most other assets that institutional investors might choose to hold, such as corporate bonds or common stock traded on major exchanges. A venture-capital investment has an investment horizon of from three to ten or more years, and the VC fund will often take a portfolio company through one or more business downturns. Individual equity investments in small firms often yield negative returns (Cochrane, 2005). For those institutional investors capable of bearing such risk and illiquidity, high expected returns are a major attraction.

Minority-oriented venture-capital funds have a mandate to invest largely in minority-owned businesses (Bates and Bradford, 2008a). Conceptually, the expected financial results for these VC funds depend significantly on whether or not minority-owned firms have full access to venture-capital funding; that is, whether majority venture-capital investors provide sufficient capital to minority-owned ventures. If minority-owned firms are treated less favorably in financial markets and have less access to venture capital than similarly situated majority businesses, then above-average returns/below average risks may be available to VC funds focused on financing minority-owned firms. Available evidence describing access to equity-capital financing, in fact, does indicate that minority owners experience less access to venture capital than nonminority owners having similar human-capital traits (Bates and Bradford, 1992). If this is indeed true, then minority-oriented venture-capital firms should achieve favorable returns in the MBE market niche because there are unmet opportunities available.

If, alternatively, minority firms have access to venture capital to the same degree as otherwise identical nonminority-owned businesses, then minority-oriented VC funds are possibly redundant because they do not have an advantageous risk/return niche in which to invest. However, the restriction to invest in minority firms can still be a successful investment strategy if the minority-oriented funds are better than other funds at identifying and screening the more successful from the less promising minority ventures. On the other hand, if minority firms have equal access to financing in mainstream financial markets and the minority funds lack greater ability to screen successful from unsuccessful ventures, then focusing on minority firms places a burden on these funds. Here the minority-oriented funds would have to invest more than an optimal portion of their portfolios in minority firms, and the funds would therefore be accepting a lower return for a given level of risk, or a higher risk for any given level of return that they achieve.

It is important to note that if a fund is restricted to invest more than an optimal portion of its assets in a given asset category, the restriction imposes an implicit tax on the institution. In the case of Specialized Small Business Investment Companies (SSBICs), the U.S. Government historically attempted to reduce the cost of this investment restriction by compensating SSBICs with subsidies. However, the SBA also imposed regulatory burdens, including frequently changing regulations, that tended to nullify these subsidy benefits (Bates, Bradford, and Rubin, 2006).

In summary, the success of minority-oriented venture-capital funds is an empirical question, because it depends on several opposing influences that are difficult to measure. If minority-owned firms are fully able to obtain financing from existing venture-capital funds, then the creation of minority-oriented venture-capital firms may not increase the amount of venture capital flowing into investment-grade minority business projects. In addition, minority-oriented venture-capital funds will not generate attractive financial returns on their investments in MBEs unless they have a greater ability than other VCs to select and invest in successful minority ventures. Fully equal access to venture capital for MBEs (in comparison to equivalent nonminority ventures) would indicate that the underserved market hypothesis is invalid simply because the minority market is not being underserved. Restricting their investments to minority-owned firms can be a cost to the minority-oriented VC funds if full and equal access to venture capital indeed describes MBEs, since the funds would be less able to take advantage of opportunities in the nonminority business sector. Absent a better ability to identify and analyze investment prospects among MBEs seeking equity capital, the minority-oriented venture-capital funds would be expected to yield lower returns and/or higher risks on investments, relative to mainstream VC funds (i.e. those not specifically targeting MBEs).

Another possibility is that minority firms do not enjoy equal access to venture-capital funds, thus allowing minority-oriented funds to earn attractive investment returns while increasing the dollar amount of equity investments received by investment-grade minority businesses. In this case, the MBE market is being underserved and the returns available to minority-oriented venture-capital funds are expected to be at least comparable to and quite possibly higher than returns generated by other venture-capital funds.

There are two direct empirical tests for the presence or absence of restricted MBE access to equity capital, the first of which entails comparing the financial performance of VC funds specializing in investing in MBEs, to the outcomes of mainstream VC funds of the same vintage (started in the same year) that do not target their investments to MBEs. The public-market-equivalent-vintage (PME-vintage) measure of VC fund investment performance is useful because it provides a direct basis for comparing the investment returns generated by minority-oriented VC funds to those produced by the mainstream VC industry. Bates and Bradford (2008a) calculated the PME-vintage measure of returns for minority-oriented VC fund investments initiated between 1989 and 1995 that had been fully realized by year end 2003, thus comparing their performance to mainstream funds of the same vintage. The PME-vintage measure was calculated by dividing the present value of minority fund cash inflows (returns) on individual equity investments by the present value of its cash outflows (investments). The discount rate used in this calculation was the equally weighted average lifetime IRRs of all private equity funds (in the Venture Economics database) of the same vintage year. This measure of investment performance is further explained in Kaplan and Schoar (2005).

This specific measure of investment returns was calculated two ways – first as an equally weighted average of individual minority-oriented VC funds' PME-vintage values (this PMEvintage value = 1.13), and secondly, as an overall PME vintage value treating all MBE-oriented funds as though they were one giant VC fund (PME-vintage value = 1.16). Either way, the minority funds outperformed mainstream funds of the same vintage. Note that a reported PME value of one would indicate that cash invested by the minority-oriented VC funds earned exactly the same returns (using IRR as the measure of returns) as equivalent cash invested into mainstream funds. A PME of less than one indicates that investing in mainstream VC funds yielded higher returns, while a PME greater than one shows that investing in the minority VC funds was the more profitable alternative. The higher returns of the minority-oriented funds are consistent with the underserved market hypothesis (Bates and Bradford, 2008a) but this conclusion must be tempered by the reality of databases that are not perfectly compatible (Venture Economics data was used to describe mainstream VC funds; survey data collected from minority-oriented VCs described these funds). Thus, the finding of higher returns for minority-oriented funds is provocative but not definitive.

An alternative test of the underserved market hypothesis requires collecting data on all realized VC investments made by a group of funds over a specific time period, all of which invested equity capital actively in MBEs, and some of which actively made VC investments in both MBE- and nonminority-owned small businesses.

The underserved market hypothesis would be supported if the observed investment returns forthcoming from realized VC investments in MBEs exceeded – to a statistically significant degree—returns from investments in the non-MBE ventures. This alternative test is presented and analyzed in this report.

C. The Nature of our Database Describing Minority-Oriented VC Funds and their Equity Investments in Small Businesses

All of the private equity funds in our database were active members of the National Association of Investment Companies (NAIC) in 2000 and/or 2003. These VCs were NAIC members because all shared an active interest in investing in MBEs. The approach used by Bates and Bradford (2003; 2008b) to generate comprehensive survey data on the minority-oriented venture-capital industry has been to work closely with this industry's dominant association, the NAIC. NAIC officials and minority VC-industry leaders aided their efforts to collect survey responses, which often involved considerable arm-twisting. Survey responses were collected from the individual minority-oriented VC funds under the sponsorship of the NAIC and a series of Kauffman Foundation-funded research projects undertaken by Timothy Bates and William Bradford over the 2001 – 2008 time period.

This database was constructed by surveying member funds at three points in time – 2001, 2004 and 2007. Not all member funds were included in our survey. A brief pre-survey of the 50 funds as of December 2000 revealed that 36 were (i) actively investing equity capital in small firms, (ii) targeting their investments largely to MBEs, and (iii) investing with a predominant focus upon generating attractive monetary returns.[2] Two funds did not respond to the pre-survey. All funds not meeting the above three conditions were dropped from further consideration. Excluded funds (12) most often were debt (as opposed to equity) oriented or were investing for social returns. All of the surveyed funds described in this study are therefore profit-oriented funds actively investing equity capital in small businesses, the majority of which are minority business enterprises (Bates and Bradford, 2003).

Based upon our pre-surveying and eligibility screening, 38 member funds were asked to complete the full survey questionnaire in 2001. Responding firms were re-surveyed in 2004 and 2007 to update investment performance information. Of the eligible funds, 24 responded to the detailed 2001 survey questionnaire (63.2 percent response rate) regarding fund traits, general partner (GP) characteristics, and monetary returns on their individual small-business investments. Further details describing the construction of this database are spelled out in the attached Appendix A: Database describing MBE-oriented VC funds and their equity investments in small businesses.

Although surveying venture-capital funds has been common since the 1980s, generating accurate, comprehensive data describing the venture-capital industry has been a huge challenge for researchers and scholars. The value of the collected data, of course, depends on the cooperation of the surveyed VC funds. Low survey response rates have been the norm. The 1995 National Census of Early-Stage Capital Financing, for example, was created by surveying 180 venture-capital firms: only 36 responded (Meyer, et al., 1995). Many academic researchers have directly surveyed venture-capital firms, notes Brophy, "but overall results were spotty, as firm partners became unwilling to disclose details for uncontrolled publication..." (1997, p.9).

The fact that NAIC member funds are united by their shared interest in investing equity capital into minority-owned businesses suggests a fundamental difference between the surveyed VC funds analyzed in this report and the rest of the U.S. venture capital industry. A demographic profile of the 41 VC fund general partners (GPs) associated with the 24 surveyed applicable funds further indicates distinctiveness, relative to the broad VC industry mainstream. Among the 41 GPs, 28 are African American, five are Asian American, three are Hispanic, and five are nonminority white. An examination of GP educational backgrounds reveals similarities with the mainstream: for the 39 GPs reporting their educational credentials, 37 held a graduate or professional degree, and 33 of those were MBA degrees. Among the institutions awarding the MBA degrees to these fund general partners, most were the nation's leading business schools, and Harvard MBA degrees were the most numerous (Bates and Bradford, 2008b). Among the 400 portfolio firms financed by the VCs described in our database, finally, owners of these ventures were most often African Americans; Hispanic-owned firms were the second most numerous; nonminority white owners were in third place and Asian owners were fourth.

D. The Demand for Venture Capital

A driving force behind rapid growth of the minority business community lies in the expanding pool of college educated, professionally trained, managerially experienced minorities seeking to start and expand large-scale businesses (Greene and Owen, 2004). Boston and Ross, observing this process in Atlanta, noted that a new African American entrepreneur has emerged. "This new entrepreneur is young, well educated, operating increasingly in non-traditional industries..." (1997, p. 339). Serving the financing needs of this new generation of high-end MBEs, minority VC funds have expanded rapidly in size and scope in recent decades (Bates & Bradford, 2003).

Gains in higher education illustrate how wider opportunities translated into significant progress in the minority business realm, permitting the "new" minority entrepreneur to emerge and become commonplace. Between 1965 and 1980, for example, minority enrollment in colleges and universities generally, and enrollment among African-Americans specifically, more than tripled (Bates, 1997a). Yet it was the qualitative change in student areas of concentration during this time period – preparing for careers in business and technical fields – that gave rise to the new African American entrepreneur (table 1). Career options widened and minority students shifted their fields of concentration dramatically to take advantage of opportunities in the business world (Bates, 1997a; Carter and Wilson, 1992; Harvey, 2003). Thus, bachelor's degrees earned by minorities since the 1970s grew most rapidly in business and engineering fields, while master's degrees saw their most rapid growth in business-related fields. By 2005, for example, over 100,000 African Americans had received MBA degrees.

The target market served by minority-oriented VC funds constitutes a small subset of the nation's minority business community. Those VC funds seeking to invest in MBEs commonly target firms whose owners have strong educational credentials and considerable managerial expertise, often acquired while working for major U.S. corporations. It is the college graduate – often the MBA recipient—who has at least ten years of work experience in corporate America who most often seeks venture capital financing for his or her growing young firm. In addition, firms receiving investments from the minority-oriented VC funds commonly have annual sales in the $1 million plus category, as well as excellent prospects for future growth in profits and sales revenues (Bates and Bradford, 2003).

Table 1. Degrees Awarded Nationwide to African Americans

A. Bachelor's degrees	1976	2000	Percent change, 1976-2000
Education	14,209	7,723	-45.9%
Business	9,489	23,645	+149.2%
Engineering	1,370	4,557	+232.6%
B. MBA degrees	1,549	8,630	+457.1%

Sources: Carter and Wilson (1992); Harvey (2003).

It is the MBEs generating annual sales of $1.0 million or more, furthermore, that create most of the employment opportunities forthcoming from the nation's steadily expanding universe of minority-owned ventures utilizing paid employees. Among black- and Hispanic-owned businesses, for example, Census Bureau data indicate that only 38,324 of the 294,000+ employer firms identified by the 2002 economic census generated annual revenues exceeding $1 million (U.S. Bureau of the Census, 2006). Yet this subset—less than one percent of all black- and Latino-owned businesses— employed 1,384,000 of the 2,291,000 workers on the payrolls of all black and Hispanic businesses in 2002 (table 2). These 38,000+ firms not only accounted for over 60 percent of all jobs generated by the nation's black and Latino business community in 2002; they also were expanding at over twice the rate of black and Hispanic firms generating under $1 million in annual sales. Helping to finance this high rate of firm growth (and job creation) is the task of the minority-oriented VC industry.

Table 2. Number of Workers Employed by Large Black- and Latino-Owned Firms in 2002 (those reporting annual sales of $1 million or more)

Race/ethnicity of firm owners:	# firms:	Total # of paid employees:
1 Large black-owned firms	10,190	446,601
2 Large Hispanic-owned firms	28,134	937,637
3 Sum of 1 and 2	38,324	1,384,238
All black/Hispanic firms with sales under $1 million	255,736	906,535

Source: U.S. Bureau of the Census Survey of Business Owners, 2006.

E. The Supply of Venture Capital

The amount and timing of investments in portfolio companies by NAIC funds is heavily shaped by the size and timing of capital investments these funds attract from institutional investors. Historically, NAIC member VC funds differed from the industry mainstream in that many were chartered by the Small Business Administration (SBA) and relied upon government as a primary funding source. Initiation of the Minority Enterprise Small Business Investment Company (MESBIC) program, administered by the SBA, in the early 1970s marked the initial creation of the minority-oriented VC fund industry (Bates, 1997b). Yet, this heritage has faded into insignificance over the past 20 years: few of the VC funds responding to our surveys were SBA chartered and fewer than 3 percent of their aggregate capitalization came from government sources other than pension funds. Dominant sources were state and local government and corporate pension funds, funds of funds, and private corporations, including banks and insurance companies (table 3). The surveyed NAIC member funds described in the VC -fund database analyzed in this report are thus properly viewed as profit-motivated investors operating on the frontiers of industry practice, drawing their funding from institutional investors expecting competitive returns.

NAIC member firms between 1989 and 1998 had, as of year end 1998, collectively raised $1.242 billion from various institutional investors. In fact, over 89 percent of that reported industry investment capital was raised from five sources (in order of importance): 1) public pension funds, 2) banks and insurance companies, 3) corporate pension funds, 4) fund of funds, and 5) the federal government (Bates and Bradford, 2003). Growth in capital resources since year end 1998 has come largely from public pension funds and funds of funds. Fund of fund financing accrued to ten of the surveyed NAIC member VC funds through year end 2004, versus four reporting such funding through year end 1998. The number of minority-oriented funds raising capital from public pension funds (table 3) more than doubled by 2004, increasing from four in 1998 to nine. Other major sources—banks, insurance companies, corporations, and corporate pension funds—have been growing slowly, relative to the two dominant institutional investors providing capital to minority-oriented private equity funds.

Growth of funds that specialize in investing equity capital in small businesses owned by minorities is driven primarily by the willingness of major institutional investors – particularly public pension funds – to commit financial capital to this traditionally neglected niche. Noteworthy in terms of timing is the inflow of capital from both public pension funds and funds of funds in the 1996-2000 period, a time period coinciding with the cyclical peak of mainstream VC industry fund raising (Bates and Bradford, 2008b). Because the minority-oriented VCs rely largely upon mainstream institutional investors seeking to earn competitive returns on their investments, the long-term viability of this sector is dependent upon the VC funds' generating investment returns sufficiently high to insure access to these funding sources in the future.

We have investigated impacts of the two dominant institutional investors – public pension-fund and funds of funds—upon the nature of the investing practices of the minority-oriented VC sector. In their role of providing well over half of all funding utilized by minority VCs to finance small businesses, these dominant institutional investors have invested in VC funds selectively.

They seek to cherry-pick the winners, investing only in the subset of minority-oriented funds poised to generate above-average financial returns for their institutional investors.

Table 3. Sources of Funding for Minority-Oriented VC Funds through Year end 2003

A. Major Sources	# funds tapping this source	Approximate range of capital raised
1.Banks, insurance cos.	15	$1 million to $45+ million
2.Fund of funds	10	$6 million to $24+ million
3.Corporations	8	$1 million to $150+ million
4.Public pension funds	9	$6 million to $100+ million
5.Misc. sources	7	$0.1 million to $25 million
6.Corporate pension funds	6	$7 million to $80 million
B. Other Sources	# of funds tapping this source	Approximate range of capital raised
1. Federal government	6	$3 million to over $17 million
2. State, local, government	2	$4 million to $5 million
3.Individuals, families	5	Under $100,000 to under $1 million
C. Median $ Amount of Capital Raised, by Selected Sources (to the nearest million)		
1 Public pension funds		$49 million
2 Fund of funds		$18 million
3 Banks, insurance cos.		$12 million
4 Corporate pension funds		$25 million
5 State, local government		$4 million
6. Federal government		$5 million
7. Corporations		$3 million
D. Total raised through year end 2003: all sources		$1,760.3 million

Source: Surveyed NAIC member funds (Bates and Bradford, 2008b).

In the process of picking and choosing those minority-oriented VC funds potentially offering the highest investment returns, the pension funds effectively shape the trajectory of this VC industry subsector. The winners—flush with funding —rapidly achieved growing prominence in the MBE equity investing realm; the losers—smaller in resources available for investing—lost relative position within the minority VC universe.

Thus shaped, minority VC funds have moved collectively toward mainstream strategies of equity investing, focusing increasingly upon financing high-tech small firms. Although still predominantly minority oriented, portfolio firms receiving these equity investments are less likely to be owned by minorities, relative to past investing patterns. We utilized logistic regression techniques to test the hypothesis that public pension funds and funds-of-funds prefer to provide funding to the minority-oriented VCs that most closely resemble the mainstream VC industry. If this hypothesis is supported by the evidence, then we have a factual basis for concluding that the mainstream investing patterns noted above that increasingly typify the MBE VC funds are being driven directly by the institutional investors' decisions to provide funding to those funds resembling mainstream VC funds.

Traits for which we have proxy variables of mainstream fund characteristics and investing practices (in our database describing minority-oriented VC funds) include the following. First, mainstream funds invest most often in hi-tech lines of business and they tend to avoid "old-economy" industries (retail, wholesale, manufacture other than hi-tech) generally (Gompers and Lerner, 1999). MBE-oriented VC funds, in contrast, have traditionally invested actively in portfolio firms operating in old-economy industries. We have industry-identifier variables for nearly 400 VC investments made by minority-oriented VC funds, allowing us to delineate VC investments in hi-tech firms from their portfolio companies operating in old-economy industries. Second, mainstream funds are largely formed by general partners possessing mainstream investment-banking work experience, often in major Wall Street institutions – Goldman Sachs, Morgan Stanley, and the like. The minority-oriented funds, in contrast, are most often formed by general partners who lack mainstream investment-banking work experience (Bates and Bradford, 2008b). We have specific measures of the types of work experience general partners of minority-oriented VC funds possessed before they became owners of their funds; thus we can identify whether or not the general partners of individual MBE VC funds had mainstream investment-banking experience prior to setting up their fund. Finally, mainstream VC funds rarely invest in MBEs; our data allow us to identify racial ownership patterns for over 300 portfolio firms in which MBE-oriented VC funds have invested.

We proceed to delineate minority-oriented VC funds tapping public pension funds and funds of funds as sources of their financial capital from those not raising institutional funding from these sources. We find that these dominant institutional funding sources indeed were more likely to provide financial capital to MBE VC funds that invested actively in white-owned business ventures (in addition to MBEs), as opposed to VC funds investing solely in MBEs. Finally, we did not detect a clear bias toward public-pension-fund investing in the VCs most oriented to investing equity capital in high-tech firms (although funds of funds do favor the hitech-oriented minority VCs), but we did find that they tended to avoid providing capital to the VC funds most actively investing in old-economy lines of business. On balance, our analysis suggests that public pension funds and funds of funds collectively do prefer to provide capital to minority VC funds investing in portfolio firms having racially diverse owners – white-owned as well as minority-owned ventures. They may indirectly encourage hi-tech investing in the sense of tending not to fund minority VCs that invest actively in old-economy lines of business.

II. ANALYSIS: EVALUATING THE VIABILITY OF THE MINORITY-ORIENTED VENTURE CAPITAL FUNDS

A. Overview

Minority-oriented venture capital funds focusing upon investing in ventures owned by African Americans and Hispanics have been increasingly investing actively in new-economy high-tech lines of business in recent years. This changing emphasis, along with a growing propensity to invest in white nonminority-owned firms, has coincided with substantial declines in the average returns generated by equity investments of minority-oriented funds. Our research has focused on understanding why minority-oriented VC funds in the 21st century increasingly invest outside of their traditional minority market niche. What are the ramifications of these investment trends for black-and Hispanic-owned ventures seeking venture capital financing? Why, finally, have the realized returns earned by the minority-oriented VC funds declined in the 21st century?

It is noteworthy that the returns on investments initiated by the minority-oriented VC funds from 1989 through year end 1995 generated by the NAIC member funds slightly exceeded those reported by the broader VC industry. Examination of the combined cash flows for realized equity investments initiated by the minority-oriented VC funds between 1989 and 1995 yielded an IRR of 17.7 percent to the institutional investors providing financial capital to these funds, while the average of the equally weighted fund IRRs was 15.4 percent (Bates and Bradford, 2008a). These 17.7 percent and 15.4 percent return figures reflect net returns to investors, after the deduction of fees charged by the VC funds and the share of profits claimed by those same funds.

Chen, Bairl, and Kaplan (2002) found an average equally weighted IRR of 13.4 percent for 148 VC funds in the Venture Economics data that had liquidated as of 1999. Ljungqvist and Richardson (2004) reported an average equally weighted IRR of 18.5 percent for 36 VC funds started in the 1989 - 1993 period. Applying the public market equivalent-vintage (PME-vintage) measure to Venture Economics data, as we previously noted, Bates and Bradford (2008a) estimated that the NAIC minority-focused funds collectively earned slightly higher returns on their realized VC investments than mainstream funds of the same vintage.

The high investment returns being generated by minority-oriented VC funds through the mid 1990s produced the unprecedented large inflow of new money raised by these funds from institutional investors – particularly pension funds – in the late 1990s. This same phenomenon of unprecedented inflows of new money, however, also characterized the mainstream venture-capital industry. There is really no such thing as a "typical year" regarding new capital resources raised by the venture-capital industry: institutional investors tend to gravitate between extremes of either pouring large amounts of new capital into VC funds or investing only small amounts, creating a feast or famine environment for the funds seeking new financial-capital resources. A comparison of the aggregate amounts of capital raised by the overall venture-capital industry in the U.S. in 1991 as opposed to 1999 is revealing. The former was a slow year: 34 new VC funds were launched nationwide with $1.69 billion in capital resources, while in 1999, over 200 funds were launched with aggregate capitalization exceeding $37 billion (Bates and Bradford, 2003).

The rapid growth of the financial resources available to the minority VC funds in the late 1990s predictably generated very large increases in their equity investments in small businesses. Bates and Bradford (2008b) estimated that the minority-oriented VC funds described in their survey (the same data source described and analyzed in this report) made new small-firm equity investments exceeding $220 million during calendar year 2000. While this dollar figure may sound low relative to the investing activities of mainstream VC funds, it is put in perspective by comparing this dollar amount to all equity investments made by these same surveyed VC funds during the entire ten-year period, 1989 to 1998: about $150 million. This large volume of top-of-the-cycle investing produced devastating consequences, particularly for the minority VC funds just getting started in 2000: realized returns for all realized investments initiated in 2000 were 2.2 percent overall through year end 2006. Returns for the year 2000 industry newcomers were even lower. Investing heavily at the VC industry's cyclical peak in 2000 is, in fact, an important factor responsible for the declining investment returns generated by minority-oriented VC funds in the 21st century.

Funds in the mainstream VC industry experienced financial returns on their equity investments initiated in 2000 quite similar to the very low returns generated by the minority-oriented funds. A near-record number of mainstream funds – 180 of them, according to Venture Economics – began investing in 2000: average realized returns on the investments initiated by these funds in 2000 were 0.5 percent through March, 2007. They outperformed the class of 1999 – the 164 equity capital funds starting to invest that year had generated a minus 2.4 percent average IRR on their VC investments through March of 2007. Venture capital investing has been a boom/bust industry for decades, complicating the efforts of funds striving to raise new capital from institutional investors in the 21st century. The minority-oriented VC funds in recent years have been heavily impacted by the same cyclical forces shaping the overall venture capital industry in the U.S. (Bates and Bradford, 2008b).

The high returns generated by VC funds in the 1990s have declined in the 21st century— both for minority funds and the broader overall mainstream U.S. venture capital industry—due, in part, to the fact that the 1990s boom years gave way to a hi-tech bubble that popped in 2000. The vibrant initial public offering (IPO) market of the 1990s – a key source of high returns for mainstream VC funds generally and minority-oriented funds specifically – subsequently stagnated. Despite the cyclical gyrations impacting the minority VC funds in recent years, the underserved market hypothesis still appears to be valid.

B. Managing the Risks Inherent in Venture Capital Investing: Strategies Employed by the Minority-Oriented Funds

To understand the investment choices made by minority VC funds, it is necessary to situate those choices in the context of the strategies these funds employ to manage successfully the considerable risks inherent in making equity investments in their portfolio firms. Investing equity capital in MBEs and other small businesses operating in a variety of industries and offering a range of equity and hybrid equity/debt financial products requires considerable depth in managerial expertise. This is less of a problem for the larger VC funds, where various general partners and staff possess a range of complementary skills. It is more of a problem for small minority-oriented funds, some of which have only one full-time manager. Indeed, several of the minority VC funds under consideration are very small by industry standards, possessing less than $10 million in total assets.

These small funds often have to struggle with lack of depth in managerial resources. Being very small, in addition, makes it difficult to achieve diversification in their portfolio of investments in small firms in an industry where such diversification is vitally important for spreading risks. A pragmatic and popular strategy in such circumstances is to invest in portfolio firms by being a participant in syndicated business investments. In fact, an outstanding feature of the minority-oriented venture-capital industry is the near universal participation of funds in syndicated investments. As a participant in syndicated deals, smaller funds can piggyback upon the expertise of the lead firm that put together the syndicated business investment. Buying a piece of a multi-million dollar venture-capital investment is a pragmatic strategy, as well, for achieving risk reduction via portfolio diversification.

Among the surveyed venture-capital funds, nearly all respondents had participated actively in syndicated business investments. An attractive opportunity, for example, to invest $ six million in equity in a promising minority business venture—absent syndication—would be overly risky for most of the minority-oriented funds. Most are simply too small to invest that amount into one firm, because an investment of that size would leave the fund under-diversified and prone to serious damage in the event of weak investment performance. Rather than losing the deal, however, the fund may choose to syndicate it, investing, perhaps, $1 million of its own funds and parceling out $ 5 million to other minority-oriented VCs. This type of syndication is widespread in the minority VC sector.

Widespread syndication is symptomatic of the extensive networking that typifies the minority-oriented venture-capital funds. Through membership in the NAIC and their frequent interaction on business investments, the general partners in this sector have developed considerable expertise in working together effectively. An important outcome has been the ability of the funds to finance larger deals while enhancing diversification of their investment portfolios. Although the minority-oriented venture-capital industry is diverse, important practices, such as syndication of investments, are quite widespread. Fund interactions with their client firms are also broadly similar among the surveyed funds. Venture-capital investing is risky. When funds purchase equity in firms that are privately held, they commonly buy into firms that are small and often young and large differences exist between what the entrepreneurs and investors know about the underlying condition of the firm.

A successful venture-capital fund must alleviate these information gaps. Tools used to achieve this involve scrutinizing firms intensely before providing equity capital and monitoring them closely afterwards. Monitoring and information tools of the venture capitalists include taking seats on the firm's board of directors, participating in long-range planning undertaken by client firms, and, when necessary, participating in the management of day-to-day operations. Syndication, in fact, should be included in this list of risk management tools used to lessen information gaps. Involving other venture funds provides a second (and third and so forth) opinion on the investment opportunity, lessening the risk that bad deals will be funded. Gompers and Lerner (1999) have shown that syndication for the purpose of getting informed opinions of investment quality is a practice often used by venture firms.

By serving on a firm's board of directors, venture-fund general partners not only learn more about the firm's operations. They also position themselves to provide advice and support for client firms. This study relied on a survey the 24 minority-oriented venture-capital funds to learn more about their interactions with client firms. Indeed, all but one of the 24 responding funds indicated that their general partners sit on the board of directors of client firms. Sitting on the board of directors, of course, facilitates participating in other aspects of client firm operations. We examined data collected from the 24 VC fund survey respondents on four kinds of general partner involvement in management of their portfolio firms: 1) advise on long-term planning, 2) assist with hiring, 3) assist in day-to-day operations, and 4) engage in active involvement in execution of exit strategy. All of the minority-oriented funds responded that they advised client firms on long-term planning and were actively involved in execution of an exit strategy.

Regarding assisting client firms with hiring, this type of general partner (GP) interaction with their clients was nearly universal; 23 of the surveyed venture funds assisted their portfolio firms thusly. Assisting in the day-to-day operations of their portfolio companies is something that many of the surveyed minority venture fund GPs did, but such assistance was the least common type of interaction between the funds and their client firms. The GPs indicate consistently that they prefer to avoid day-to-day involvement in managing their portfolio companies, ideally leaving such operations decision-making in the hands of company managers. Indeed, not all GPs have the necessary expertise to benefit portfolio companies by being actively involved in portfolio company operating decisions. Being an effective GP in this context commonly requires a degree of both experience and expertise that is time-consuming, expensive, and generally difficult to obtain, which is why a key constraint on the ability of VC funds to invest profitably is a constrained supply of appropriately skilled and talented GPs (Gompers and Lerner, 1999). An important finding – discussed later in this report – is that minority fund GP involvement in day-to-day operational decision-making with their portfolio companies is associated positively with earning higher rates of return on their realized equity investments, in comparison with funds not active in such day-to-day operations.

Because endogeneity is potentially present in the relationship between GP activism and the realized value of portfolio firm investments, survey questions on activism were designed to mitigate such problems. Our concern is that if fund GPs adjust their behavior when individual portfolio companies do well, paying more attention to the strong performers, a positive association between GP activism and investment performance may be observed, but such activism does not necessarily enhance performance. Thus, the activism survey questions were designed to conform to an ex ante, systematic treatment of portfolio companies. The questions were asked to elicit responses about the average level of activism across all of the firms in the VC's portfolio. This helps to mitigate the problem of endogeneity of activism as an explanatory variable in regression models explaining IRRs values. Our measure of activism is fund specific instead of project specific. Effectively, our VC-specific measure of activism becomes an instrument for activism at the project level (Jackson, Bates and Bradford, forthcoming).

One of the most fundamental strategic questions that venture-capital fund managers must face, finally, is whether to diversify across a range of different industries and markets or to specialize in particular markets. Proponents of diversification argue that there are substantial gains from leveraging managerial skills and abilities across industries and geographic markets. These gains may originate from the spreading of fixed costs over additional investments through economies of scale. On the other hand, proponents of a focused strategy for VC funds argue that diversification will dilute the current competitive advantage of management by pushing managers beyond their existing expertise and capabilities. Thus, the question of whether diversification improves the performance of VC funds in general, and minority-oriented VC funds in particular, may be answered only through empirical analysis. Norton and Tenenbaum (1993) report evidence that is more supportive of a focused strategy for VC funds. Sah and Stiglitz (1986) and Admati and Pfleider (1994) suggest that involvement in syndicated transactions can spread portfolio risks and provide other benefits of diversification by providing better information for investment decision-making, and a means of signaling value.

The minority funds, by way of summary, seek to minimize the risks associated with investing equity capital in their portfolio of business ventures by participating actively in syndication of their small firm investments. Second, nearly all of the fund general partners actively participate in the affairs of their portfolio companies – sitting on boards of directors and involving the VC general partners in such managerial functions as assistance with hiring, engaging in active day-by-day managerial decision making, and participating in long-run planning. Regarding types of GP interaction with their client firms, importantly, substantial variation across funds was present only in the "assist in day-to-day operations" category. Finally, the minority-oriented VC funds, instead of focusing narrowly on a single industry, often rely on a diverse industry mix of portfolio companies; they are typically are more broadly diversified than the majority venture-capital industry.

Table 4. Summary Statistics, Investments Realized through Year end 2006

Variable:	Mean	Median	Standard Deviation	Minimum	Maximum
IRR-all investments (equally weighted)	-0.20	-0.01	0.69	-1.00	3.21
Old-generation fund	0.88	1.00	0.33	0.00	1.00
Log of investment	12.86	12.79	1.54	8.39	17.22
Total investment $ amount ($000)	1,581.4	616.5	3,028.5	10.0	30,000.00
Initial Year Investment ($000)	1,248.8	360.00	3,028.4	4.41	30,000.00
High tech	0.21	0.18	0.16	0.00	0.58
Communications	0.45	0.42	0.31	0.00	1.00
Medical services	0.03	0.00	0.05	0.00	0.17
Old economy	0.18	0.16	0.16	0.00	1.00
Year of investment, 1999 or 2000	0.27	0.00	0.44	0.00	1.00
Investments Per GP	10.09	7.67	6.41	1.00	21.67
Activism	0.84	1.00	0.37	0.00	1.00
Minority Firm	0.90	1.00	0.30	0.00	1.00
N= 303					

C. Understanding the Minority-Oriented VC Funds and their Equity Investments in Small-Business Ventures: Descriptive Statistics

We present summary statistics in table 4 describing characteristics of the minority- oriented VC funds under consideration, the types of firms in which they invest, and the strategies they use in their quest for generating high returns on their equity investments in portfolio firms. Table 4 statistics also describe certain traits of the 303 realized small-business equity investments made by the surveyed minority-oriented VC funds. Information about the characteristics of our variables is provided in Appendix B, Variable definitions.

The "old-generation fund" variable (table 4) captures an important phenomenon that requires clarification. Discussions with leaders in the minority VC sector, including past board chairmen of the NAIC, point toward an old generation, new generation dichotomy among the general partners of minority-oriented VC funds. General partners organizing and operating newer second-generation equity funds tend to be graduates of the nation's top MBA programs who began their careers working for major Wall Street investment banks. Reflecting their training and work experience at those large institutions and their professional networks in the world of finance, they created private-equity-investing funds that often resembled those formed by whites.

When general partners of these second-generation funds search for opportunities to invest equity capital in small businesses, they typically tap professional networks that are racially diverse and their deal flow is similarly diverse. Work experience acquired prior to creating their own funds typically exposed them to clients and colleagues as racially diverse as clients and colleagues at leading giant investment banks generally. Predictably, they create funds that often invest in high-tech companies, many of which are not minority owned. Second-generation funds, finally, have enjoyed greater access to public pension fund capital than older first generation veterans.

General partners of the first-generation funds were often founding members of the NAIC; they are the pioneers who created the minority-oriented venture-capital industry back in the 1970s and 1980s. Many of these industry veterans feel a sense of commitment to alleviate the restricted access to investment capital that has traditionally handicapped MBEs. Indeed, some express little interest in funding the equity-capital needs of the nonminority-owned firms. Their objective is to generate high financial returns for their funds by investing in MBEs having limited access to mainstream sources of equity capital. Their work experience prior to becoming partners in private equity funds rarely included stints in large investment banks. Their deal flows originate mostly in their professional networks, which produce potential clients who are typically MBEs, often operating in old-economy lines of business.

The above discussion suggests that no single minority-oriented private equity fund group exists but, rather, two branches pursue distinct investing strategies. While their strategies do differ, it is nonetheless important to recognize that both the old and the new generation are devoted to generating high financial returns on their equity investments in small businesses. The second-generation funds thus invest actively in MBEs running old-economy businesses when they encounter profitable deals and the first-generation funds have increased their investment diversity in response to opportunities.

Table 4's old-generation fund mean value indicates that 88 percent (by number) of the 303 realized equity investments made by the VC funds were undertaken by old-generation funds. The newer funds – those formed since 1998—have been active investors as well but many of their outstanding equity investments have not yet been fully realized and are therefore excluded from consideration; note that the unrealized and partially realized equity investments are, however, included in the table 7 summary statistics reported below.

Table 4 summary statistics describing types of industries in which VC investments have been made indicate that communications firm investments (mean value of .45) were the most common type of equity investment made by the minority-oriented VC funds over the applicable 1989 through 2006 period; investments in high-tech (variable mean of .21) ventures ranked second. Note that the .21 mean value refers not simply to the frequency of hi-tech investments by the VC funds under consideration but, more accurately, the proportion of their total equity investments (dollar amounts) in portfolio companies the VC funds have invested in hi-tech deals. Beyond these two industry groups, means describing other industry groups – medical services, old-economy fields (including manufacturing unrelated to hi-tech, wholesale, and retail) – suggest that minority-oriented VC funds are widely diversified regarding industry distribution of their investments.

Average sizes of the realized VC investments made by the minority-oriented funds are described in table 4 in several ways. The "total investment" summary statistics indicate that the average dollar amount among the applicable 303 realized equity investments was $1.581 million and the median amount was $616.5 thousand. These are large investments being made in portfolio firms, most of which are multi-million dollar enterprises in terms of their annual sales revenues. The smaller median – as opposed to mean – investment size reflects both the wide variance in dollar amounts among these equity investments and the fact that some of them are quite large, sometimes exceeding $5 million, a substantial amount of equity to be investing in a single small business venture. The trend in recent years among the minority VCs has been towards funding larger and larger equity investments in their portfolio companies. Corresponding mean values among the equity investments initially made by these VC funds during the 1989 through 1995 period were under

$600,000 (Bates and Bradford, 2008a). Some equity investments are made in stages, which explains why the average "initial year investment" amount was $1.249 million, and the corresponding median was $360.0 thousand (table 4). Particularly when investments are made in younger portfolio firms, follow-up investments in the same company are sometimes added in later years, depending upon the progress the applicable portfolio firm is making toward goals acceptable to the investing VC fund.

"Activism" in table 4's statistics is defined as a measure of GP involvement in the day-to-day operations of their portfolio companies. An activism mean value of .84 indicates that 84 percent of the 303 realized equity investments were made by VC funds that actively involve themselves from time to time in the daily operational management of their portfolio companies. Three common rationales exist for a venture capitalist to become active in the day-to-day operations of a portfolio company. First, the company may experience unforeseen major operating problems. Second, the company may experience unforeseen major opportunities. Finally, in the inevitable event of such unforeseen problems and/or opportunities arising periodically, this particular venture capitalist may have more ability to assist portfolio companies than other VC general partners not choosing to involve themselves in the day-to-day operations of their portfolio companies. Rationales one and two are project specific and generally relate to *ex post* investment circumstances. However, rationale three entails a systematic difference across venture capital firms, and often relates to *ex ante* investment circumstances, or investment strategies. The type of activism we are measuring here is concerned with the third rationale, varying levels of GP ability across funds.

The .27 mean value of the "year of investment, 1999 or 2000" variable (table 4) indicates that 27 percent (82 actual investments) of the 303 realized investments made by the minority-oriented VC funds under consideration were initially funded in either 1999 or 2000). Prior to 1996, these same VC funds rarely made as many as 20 new equity investments in small businesses in any single given year. The 1999, 2000 period was by far the most active time period regarding new VC investments being initiated during the entire 1989 to 2006 investing period analyzed in this report.

Making equity investments and then monitoring portfolio companies after funding has been disbursed are time-consuming activities for the general partners of the minority-oriented VC funds. The mean value of 10.09 for "investments per GP" indicates that, on average, there are ten-plus realized equity investments for each VC fund general partner. Finally, the "minority firm" mean value of .90 reported in table 4 indicates that 90 percent of the 303 equity investments described were made to portfolio firms owned by minorities.

Table 5. Correlations Matrix (Select Variables) N=303

Variable	IRR	Old-generation fund	Log of invest-ment	Syndi-cated	High tech	Commu-nications	Year of invest-ment 1999 or 2000	Invest-ments Per GP	Acti-vism	Minori-ty Firm
IRR	1.00									
Old-genera-tion fund	-0.04	1.00								
Log of invest-ment	0.03	-0.45**	1.00							
Syndi-cated	-0.06	0.32**	-0.09	1.00						
High tech	0.03	0.01	-0.05	0.07	1.00					
Commu-nica-tions	-0.10	0.15*	-0.04	0.21**	-0.64**	1.00				
Year of invest-ment, 1999 or 2000	-0.30**	-0.23**	0.14*	-0.01	-0.05	-0.05	1.00			
Invest-ments Per GP	0.18**	0.36**	-0.39**	0.03	0.46**	-0.41**	-0.20**	1.00		
Acti-vism	0.11	0.22**	-0.09	0.31**	-0.17**	0.19**	0.06	0.13*	1.00	
Minori-ty Firm	0.05	0.28**	-0.34**	0.19**	0.07	0.22**	-0.10	0.08	-0.02	1.00

A correlations matrix is presented (table 5) depicting interrelationships among variables describing both VC fund traits and the fully realized equity investments under consideration. Particularly noteworthy is the fact that the "minority firm" variable is positively correlated to old-generation fund, syndicated, and communications variables, but negatively correlated to investment dollar amount, in comparison to VC investments in ventures owned by whites. One clear implication is that portfolio firms owned by minorities typically receive smaller equity investments (than white-owned ventures), and these investments are relatively more frequently made by old-generation VC funds. Second, VC investments in minority-owned portfolio firms are more often syndicated than the investments the VC funds make in white-owned businesses. Last, equity investments in communications firms are disproportionately made to MBE-owned (as opposed to white-owned) communications companies. Stated differently, VC-fund investments in white-owned portfolio firms are positively correlated to new-generation VC funds, larger investment dollar amounts, and non-syndicated investments; VC investments in white-owned ventures, furthermore, are negatively correlated to the communications company variable.

D. Regression Analysis of the Financial Returns Generated by VC-Fund Realized Investments

We next investigate the question, what characteristics and actions of the minority-oriented VC funds, and what portfolio company traits predict IRR values for individual realized venture-capital investments in specific portfolio firms. By way of summary, multiple major changes swept through the minority-oriented equity-capital-investing funds since the mid-1990s, and the task of regression analysis is to differentiate the more from the less important of these changes. A number of new VC funds were started up and had begun investing during the1999 through 2001 period. Large-scale investment of public pension fund resources helped to fuel rapid growth of private equity investing among the minority-oriented funds. Average sizes of the equity investments being made in portfolio companies have increased substantially. A new generation of general partners entered into this industry segment in the late 1990s, bringing with them investment strategies that produced expanded equity investment into high-tech lines of business. Along with this growth of high-tech investing was the growth of equity investments by minority-oriented funds into firms owned by white nonminorities. Thus, growth of number of VC funds, fund resources, and new types of investment emphasis all became major new developments shaping this sector since the late 1990s. One task of regression analysis is to differentiate the more from the less important of these changes.

We use a generalized least squares (GLS) random effects regression model to predict IRR values for the 303 realized investments in portfolio companies initially funded by the minority-oriented VCs during the 1989 – 2004 period. The GLS random effects regressions adjust the estimated coefficients and standard errors for the interrelationships among investments of the same fund (22 funds made 303 investments). This particular GLS process also adjusts for the response rate associated with our sample, allowing for better predictions about the population from which the sample was drawn.

Based on the findings of Bates and Bradford (2008a) and other studies, our regression analyses include various explanatory variables recognized in the scholarly literature as factors shaping financial returns on the realized venture-capital investments of portfolio companies, including: 1) old-generation fund dummy, 2) log of investment size, 3) proportion of investments syndicated, 4) proportion of VC fund investments in high-tech portfolio companies and other common industry groups appearing in VC-fund investment portfolios, including communications, medical services, and old-economy fields; 5) year of investment, 1999 or 2000 dummy, 6) investments per GP, 7) GP activism in the affairs of portfolio companies, and 8) an MBE portfolio firm indicator variable.

1. Hypothesized Relationships between Explanatory Variables and IRR Values

a. Minority Firm:
We expect that equity investments in minority-owned portfolio firms are likely to yield higher returns, other factors being constant, than investments in ventures owned by nonminoritywhites. We hypothesize, in other words, that MBEs seeking equity capital from VC funds do so in an underserved market environment, and the reality of this market being underserved is the reason why VC funds can earn higher returns in this market segment. Findings of Bates and Bradford (2008a) that minority-oriented VCs earned high returns on their equity investments in MBEs initiated during the 1989 through 1995 time period is consistent with the existence of an underserved VC market.

b. Proportion of VC Fund Investments in High-Tech Portfolio Companies and other Select Industries
We have no a priori expectations of likely returns available from investing in communications, medical services, or old-economy lines of business (retail, wholesale, manufacturing other than hi-tech) or miscellaneous industry groups, as opposed to high-tech lines of business. We define high-tech as software, information technology, and computer-related electronics manufacturing.

c. Old-Generation Fund Dummy

Several minority VC funds were started in the late 1990s and thereafter by newcomers possessing different human-capital characteristics than minority-oriented fund GPs have possessed traditionally. The general partners of these new funds may have an advantage over those in older funds as the latter entered the VC industry lacking prior experience in investment banking, while many of the former worked in mainstream investment banking institutions prior to their entry into this VC industry sector. On one hand, their work experience in investment banking and resulting professional networks may convey investing advantages. Conversely, this new generation of fund managers is less familiar with investing in the underserved markets that have been the traditional deal source for minority-oriented funds. This variable is equal to one if the VC fund began operations before 1998, zero otherwise. We do not have priors about whether this factor impacts realized investment returns positively or negatively.

d. Log of Investment Size

Bates and Bradford (2008a) found that larger investment size predicted higher returns, other factors being equal. Consistent with these results, we hypothesize a positive relationship between individual investment size and realized returns. Our specific measure of investment size utilized in regression analyses is the natural log of total first-year cash flow invested by the VC into the portfolio company; note that this is a portfolio-company-specific trait (as opposed to a fund-specific trait).

e. Year of Investment, 1999 or 2000 Dummy

We hypothesize that investments initiated in the peak years in the VC funding boom of the late 1990s – 1999 and 2000 – produce lower returns than investments initiated before or after the peak, other things being equal. Intense competition among equity-investing funds bid up the prices of portfolio companies, and our discussions with NAIC fund general partners indicate that these rich prices peaked in 2000 and then broke in 2001 (Bates and Bradford, 2008b). This variable, which is portfolio-company specific, is calculated as an indicator variable equal to one if the investment was initiated in either the years 1999 or 2000, zero otherwise.

f. Proportion of Investments Syndicated

Our next explanatory variable measures the degree of fund participation in syndication of investments. Involvement in syndicated transactions can provide better investment decisions, diversification, and a means of signaling value (Admati and Pfleider, 1994). Nonetheless, the funds originating most of the syndicated investments may keep the best investments entirely for themselves, or, alternatively, syndicate large investments without respect to quality to diversify their portfolios broadly (Brander, Amit, and Antweiler, 2002). Thus, we do not have priors about whether this factor impacts realized investment returns positively or negatively.

g. Activism

VC general partners provide direct managerial services and support to their portfolio companies (Sapienza, 1992). Hellman and Puri (2002) suggest that these managerial services and support create value partly by "professionalizing" the portfolio firms of VCs. In these ways, VCs exert costly efforts to improve their investment outcomes (Kaplan and Stromberg, 2004). In our regression model, the activism variable (assist in day-to-day operations) is an indicator variable equal to one if the level of activity is reported as undertaken sometimes, and zero if the level of activity is reported as never. We therefore hypothesize that GP activism is associated with increased returns on realized investments. Note that this is a fund-specific trait.

h. Investments per GP

The concept of an optimal portfolio size for a VC fund is rooted in the notion that GPs create value when they assist their portfolio companies. Yet a tradeoff exists between the number of portfolio firms in which a VC fund invests and the advisory effort that can be allocated to these businesses. Too many portfolio companies may cause GP efforts to be stretched too thinly, thus diluting the value of their assistance and lessening VC fund financial returns on their venture capital investments (Jackson et al., forthcoming). Because we are unsure of the optimal number of portfolio fund investments per GP, we have no priors about how the number of investments per GP impact IRR values.

2) Regression Analysis Findings

We turn to identifying, with regression analysis techniques, the fund traits and strategies that predict high investment returns among the realized VC investments of the minority-focused VC funds, in light of the wide variance in returns across those funds. Thus, we conduct statistical tests to determine the fund characteristics that are correlated with the IRR values of individual VC investments in firms. What profiles and strategies typify the more successful, as opposed to the less successful funds? We use the IRR of individual realized equity investments as the dependent variable in our regression analysis, i.e., our measure of fund performance.

Table 6. GLS Random Effects Regression Models Explaining Relationships between IRR Values of Realized Investments and Traits of VC Funds and their Portfolio Firms

Model	1		2	
Variable	Coefficient	T-ratio	Coefficient	T-ratio
Constant	-0.04	-0.11	-0.16	-0.38
Old-generation fund	-0.42**	-5.57	-0.42**	-5.50
Log of investment	0.01	0.51	0.02	0.91
Syndicated	-0.13	-1.35	-0.20*	-2.00
High tech	-0.37	-1.45	-0.50	-1.89
Communications	-0.19	-1.01	-0.36	-1.74
Medical services	1.37**	2.77	1.00	1.92
Old economy	-0.16	-0.59	-0.35	-1.21
Year of investment, 1999 or 2000	-0.51**	-10.43	-0.51**	-10.33
Investments Per GP	0.02**	4.68	0.02**	4.50
Activism	0.26**	4.22	0.31**	4.82
Minority Firm	---		0.21**	3.12
N= 303				
Adj-R^2	0.14		0.14	
F-statistic	25.68**		24.26**	

** significant at the one percent level or better
* significant at the 5 percent level or better.
Robust standard errors are utilized.

Turning to table 6's regression findings, the coefficient values identify VC fund and portfolio company traits associated with generating higher (or lower) investment returns, measured by IRR values for realized investments. Higher IRR values are associated (table 6, model two) with 1) investing in MBEs, 2) activism in assisting portfolio companies on the part of the VC fund general partners, and 3) a larger number of VC investments per fund general partner. It is noteworthy that all of these traits linked to higher returns on realized investments represent investing strategies employed at the discretion of the individual VC funds. Lower IRR values are associated with 1) making investments in white-owned firms, 2) being an old-generation fund, 3) participating in syndicated investments, and 4) top-of-the-cycle investing (making investments initially funded in either 1999 or 2000). Investing in high-tech companies, according to the regression analysis findings, does not appear to be a productive strategy for minority-oriented VC funds seeking to generate high financial returns on their realized investments.

Table 6's regression findings clearly validate the underserved minority market hypothesis: investing in MBEs, other factors constant, generates higher returns for the minority VCs than investments in nonminority-owned ventures. In English, "other factors constant" means that investments of the exact same dollar amount, initiated in the same time period, by minority-oriented VC funds using identical strategies regarding such factors as syndication, investment by industry, GP activism with portfolio companies, and the like, produced higher IRR values if the company was minority owned and lower values if the company was white owned. Among two portfolio companies alike in terms of all factors under consideration, other that race of owners, the minority-owned portfolio company generated higher measured returns than the nonminority-owned company, and this difference is statistically significant among the 303 investments under consideration (table 6).

Additionally, regression analysis findings indicate that investing actively in hi-tech lines of business is associated with lower investment returns, but this relationship is only borderline statistically significant. Similarly, the traditional industry in which minority-oriented VCs have invested most heavily – communications – also generated lower returns on realized investments, but the lack of statistical significance prevents us from concluding that communications investments yield systematically lower returns, relative to realized investments in miscellaneous industries (the excluded comparison group). Investments in old-economy lines of business generated yields on realized investments broadly similar to those in communications fields. Medical services, in contrast, appear to offer attractive returns relative to the kinds of industries (communications, hi-tech) where VC investments are most often made; this relationship was borderline statistically significant.

The GLS regression analysis findings indicate as well that investing equity capital into portfolio firms in 1999 and 2000 – investing at the very top of the VC industry's boom/bust cycle – generated large drops in realized investment returns. The reality of sharply lower IRR values being explained by top-of-the-cycle investing (table 6) is quite important. Investments initially funded in the years 1999 or 2000 by the minority-oriented funds under consideration produced much lower IRRs, other factors constant, than investments initiated before or after 1999 and 2000; this difference in investment returns is statistically highly significant. Investing heavily at the top of a boom/bust cycle, while certainly a negative, is perhaps a transitory phenomenon rather than a strategy likely to indicate enduring returns on the investments realized by the minority-oriented VC funds.

Also quite noteworthy is the regression analysis finding that new-generation funds – those established by newcomers entering the industry between 1999 and 2001 – earned higher IRRs on realized investments, when other factors are controlled for (table 6). Yes, they often invested in portfolio companies at the top of the cycle and they often invested in nonminority-owned firms, but regression analysis controls for these other factors. Isolating the influence of the "new-generation" trait from year of investment initiation and the other table 6 explanatory variables, being a new-generation fund – holding other factors constant – is associated with higher IRR values, and this difference in returns is statistically significant, suggesting that the specific human-capital traits of the newcomers to the minority-oriented segment of the VC industry – mainstream investment banking working experience – conveyed investing advantages.

It is noteworthy that non-syndicated investments outperformed syndicated ones (table 6), which suggests that VC funds are increasingly keeping their most promising investments entirely for themselves, while syndicating the less promising deals in order to spread the risk of a poor ultimate outcome for these deals. Not syndicating venture capital investments is a growing trend in the broader mainstream VC industry. Additionally, investments by funds that were highly active with portfolio firms had higher IRRs, other things equal. This finding was robust across alternative specifications of the activity level explanatory variable. VC funds having a larger number of investments per general partner also generated higher investment returns, but the positive impact of a higher number of investments per GP was small in magnitude. All of the factors discussed above – syndication, activism, and number of investments per GP – were correlated to realized investment returns in a statistically significant manner. In contrast, the relationship between investment size and investment IRR values was small and statistically insignificant.

Emerging from the regression analyses discussed above are traits associated with minority-oriented VC fund investing that produced high realized investment returns. In terms of strategy, higher returns are earned by funds 1) investing in minority-owned companies, and 2) involving general partners actively in assisting their portfolio companies. Strategy alone did not completely explain IRR variance patterns: minority-oriented funds unfortunate enough to be actively investing in portfolio companies in the peak years of

1999 and 2000 produced sharply lower IRRs, in comparison to their investments initiated in off-peak years.

New-generation funds, finally, emerged as particularly successful investors when other factors are controlled for. A profile of funds earning lower returns also emerges from the regression analyses: old-generation funds making syndicated investments in portfolio firms – especially nonminority white-owned ventures—are underperformers, especially if the GPs are not highly active in assisting their portfolio companies. Minority-oriented funds often possess a mix of these positive and negative traits, which is precisely why we have utilized regression analysis techniques to sort out the complex interactions between relevant traits and investment performance.

Portfolio company industry of operation did not emerge from the table 6 regression analysis as a major determinant of portfolio firm investment performance. The evidence points toward investments in hi-tech ventures as the least promising, in terms of portfolio firm industry orientation, for making equity investments in small business ventures. In terms of investing strategy, medical services stands out as the single industry group most strongly correlated to higher returns on realized investments.

iii. Adding Unrealized and Partially Realized Investments into the Analysis of the Viability of the Minority-Oriented vc Industry

The above discussion excludes from consideration all VC investments initiated by the MBE-oriented funds between 1989 and 2004 that had not been fully realized by year end 2006. In this section, the 85 investments initiated during these years which were either unrealized or only partially realized by year end 2006 are considered, in addition to the fully realized VC investments in portfolio companies. Table 7 provides summary statistics describing the applicable 303 realized investments, combined with the 85 not fully realized VC investments. A comparison of the mean and median values of the various variables in this combined sample (reported in table 7) identifies – in conjunction with table 4's summary statistics describing the 303 realized investments, certain broad trends that appear to be gradually changing the nature of the minority-oriented VC industry. The old-generation funds, of course, are gradually losing their dominance in this industry subsector: table 4's statistics included only 36 VC investments initiated by new-generation VC funds; table 7, in contrast, includes 62 such investments.

As the investments initiated by new-generation funds become relatively more numerous, a comparison of the table 4 and 7 summary statistics for certain variables point toward emerging investing trends characterizing the minority-oriented funds. Relative to table 4 statistics, table 7 mean and median statistics highlight 1) the increasing size (measured by log of investment) of individual VC investments in portfolio companies. Further, high-tech investments are rising in relative frequency while VC investments in firms operating in communications and old-economy fields are declining. Further, GP activism is gradually increasing in relative frequency and numbers of investments per GP are declining. One noteworthy omission from table 7 is summary statistics describing the relative frequency of minority-owned portfolio firms; they are excluded because we have no information on the minority-ownership status of VC investments that are not fully realized.

Table 7. Summary Statistics, Realized, Partially Realized, and Unrealized Investments through Year end 2006

Variable:	Mean	Median	Std. Dev.	Minimum	Maximum
IRR-all investments (equally weighted)	-0.20	0.00	0.64	-1.00	3.21
Old-generation fund	0.84	1.00	0.37	0.00	1.00
Log of investment	13.04	13.12	1.55	8.39	17.22
Syndicated	0.92	1.00	0.23	0.00	1.00
High tech	0.22	0.25	0.17	0.00	0.62
Communications	0.43	0.42	0.31	0.00	1.00
Medical services	0.03	0.00	0.05	0.00	0.17
Old economy	0.17	0.16	0.16	0.00	1.00
Year of investment, 1999 or 2000	0.26	0.00	0.44	0.00	1.00
Investments Per GP	9.91	7.00	6.48	1.00	21.67
Activism	0.85	1.00	0.36	0.00	1.00
N= 388					

Table 8's regression analysis of IRR values attached to the 388 investments in portfolio companies (described in table 7) entailed adding the 85 unrealized investments and replicating the earlier table 6 regression analysis explaining the IRR dependent variable; this exercise provides a crude robustness check of our previous regression findings of IRR determinants. If the regression analysis outcomes were to change radically when unrealized investments are included, one would tend to doubt the validity of the whole table 6 regression exercise. The unrealized and partially realized equity investments are now included, causing the sample size to increase from 303 observations to 388, and the returns attached to these additions reflect not the judgment of the marketplace but the subjective judgment of the VC fund itself as to what each individual unrealized investment is actually worth. Given the extremely subjective nature of attaching dollar valuations to unrealized (and partially realized) VC investments, one must take the regression findings less seriously than their table 6 counterparts. Nonetheless, there should be more noise and less precision in table 8's regression findings, but no dramatic changes. Fortunately, that is exactly what these regression findings indicate.

Table 8. GLS Random Effects Regression Models Explaining Relationships between IRR Values of Realized, Partially Realized, and Unrealized Investments and Traits of VC Funds and their Portfolio Firms

Model	1		2	
Variable	Coefficient	T-ratio	Coefficient	T-ratio
Constant	-0.12	-0.36	-0.25	-0.73
Old-generation fund	-0.38**	-6.91	-0.38**	-6.88
Log of investment	0.00	0.15	0.01	0.42
Syndicated	-0.17*	-2.23	-0.20**	-2.67
High tech	-0.09	-0.44	-0.15	-0.79
Communications	0.07	0.51	0.00	0.01
Medical services	1.24**	2.81	1.06*	2.37
Old economy	0.12	0.68	0.07	0.38
Year of investment, 1999 or 2000	-0.47**	-11.33	-0.47**	-11.18
Investments Per GP	0.02**	3.81	0.02**	3.71
Activism	0.30**	5.75	0.32**	6.15
Minority Firm	---	---	0.16*	2.52
N= 388				
Adj-R^2	0.12		0.12	
F-statistic	25.64**		24.63**	

** significant at the one percent level or better
* significant at the 5 percent level or better.
The Aldrich-Nelson goodness of fit measure is reported.

E. Is the Treatment of MBE Portfolio Funds Impacted by VC-Fund Equity Capital Investments in Nonminority-Owned Business Ventures?

Questions considered in this section are whether diversifying outside the underserved minority market niche increases or decreases the quality of the management support services and the amount of equity capital minority-oriented VC funds provide to their portfolio of minority-owned small businesses. The issue of interest is whether diversification into nonminority investments by minority-oriented VC funds has helped or hurt access of MBEs to equity capital and support from fund general partners. We recognize that investing a portion of VC-fund equity capital in nonminority-owned small business ventures does not necessarily equate to investing less equity capital in minority-owned firms. If, for example, diversification into nonminority investing allows minority-oriented VC funds to grow relatively more rapidly, then diversification may actually increase the absolute size of the potential pool of investable funds available to these funds to invest in MBEs.

Additionally, diversification into nonminority investing may increase the number of syndication opportunities available to the minority-oriented VC funds. More syndication participation may strengthen the professional and social networks of the minority-oriented VC fund. And stronger professional and social networks may increase the overall quality of the managerial services that the minority-oriented VC fund may offer when investing in MBEs. In the final analysis, whether diversification into nonminority investments by minority-oriented VC funds improves the access of minority-owned small businesses to the equity capital market is an empirical question.

In table 9's regression analysis, the issue of interest is this: does greater VC fund investing in firms owned by nonminority whites impact activism on the part of fund general partners in ways that might harm minority-owned portfolio companies? The answer, according to our regression findings, is yes, possibly. The regression analysis dependent variable (table 9) is an activism measure, indicating whether the VC fund general partners become involved in the day-to-day management decisions of the companies in their portfolio of VC investments. This is important because, as the findings of table 6's regression analysis indicated, activism on the part of the VC fund's general partners is associated positively with increased returns on the fund's realized investments. Stated differently, activism on the part of the general partners adds value to the fund's investments in portfolio companies.

The minority-oriented VC funds that invest more frequently in white-owned companies engage in activist efforts to assist their portfolio companies more often than funds not investing in firms owned by non-Hispanic whites. Thus, they are adding value to their portfolio companies, which include a mix of MBEs and white-owned firms, more so than their counterparts not investing outside of the MBE client pool. These same findings hold up, as well, when unrealized investments are added into the regression analysis portfolio company sample (regression results not reported). We conclude that GP activist involvement in the management of its portfolio companies impacts MBEs in diverse ways. These more activist funds with GPs who are willing to participate in day-to-day management decision making with their portfolio companies would undoubtedly be benefitting more minority-owned portfolio companies if they chose to invest in fewer white-owned ventures, but the countervailing fact is that VC funds entirely oriented toward MBE investing are less likely than their counterparts to intervene as actively in day-to-day management decision making with their portfolio firms.

Table 9. Logit Regression Models Explaining Relationships between Activism by VC Fund General Partners and Traits of VC Funds and their Portfolio Firms (Realized Investments Only)

Model	1		2	
Variable	Coefficient	T-ratio	Coefficient	T-ratio
Constant	-11.81**	-3.59	-11.61**	-3.26
Old-generation fund	-0.74	-1.03	0.05	0.07
Log of investment	0.25	1.60	0.15	0.87
Syndicated	4.39**	4.73	5.17**	5.51
High tech	2.98	1.34	6.48**	2.52
Communications	6.73**	3.81	10.47**	4.76
Medical services	16.54**	3.32	30.80**	3.77
Old economy	9.71**	3.04	12.99**	3.84
Year of investment, 1999 or 2000	0.64	1.30	0.78	1.45
Investments Per GP	0.14**	2.92	0.20**	3.66
Minority Firm	---	---	-4.49**	-3.61
N= 303				
Pseudo-R^2	0.20		0.25	

** significant at the one percent level or better.
* significant at the 5 percent level or better.
The Aldrich-Nelson goodness of fit measure is reported.

A related question concerns possible differences in the behavior among old-generation as opposed to new-generation VC funds regarding active general partner involvement in assisting their MBE portfolio companies. The old-generation funds have more consistently maintained their focus upon their traditional minority clientele, relative to the new-generation funds. We test in table 10's regression analysis whether GP involvement in day-to-day management of minority-owned portfolio companies differs across the groups of old- and new-generation funds, other factors being equal. This is done by re-estimating table 9's logistic regression exercise solely for the 273 realized VC investments in MBE portfolio companies. Formally, our hypothesis is that old-generation fund general partners, other factors being constant, are more likely than new-generation VC fund GPs to involve themselves in day-to-day management affairs of their MBE portfolio companies. The positive and statistically significant regression coefficient attached to the old-generation fund explanatory variable (table 10) is consistent with this hypothesis.

Table 10. Logit Regression Models Explaining Relationships between Activism by VC Fund General Partners and Traits of VC Funds and their Portfolio Firms Owned by Minorities (Realized Investments Only)

Variable	Coefficient	T-ratio
Constant	-22.62**	-4.14
Old-generation fund	1.78*	2.12
Log of investment	0.12	0.62
Syndicated	6.28**	5.92
High tech	14.51**	3.58
Communications	14.76**	4.51
Medical services	58.65**	4.05
Old economy	14.01**	3.67
Year of investment, 1999 or 2000	0.51	0.87
Investments Per GP	0.22**	4.33
N= 273		
Pseudo-R2	0.28	

** significant at the one percent level or better.
* significant at the 5 percent level or better.
Robust standard errors are utilized.

A broadly related issue is whether MBE portfolio companies receive investments that are smaller in dollar amount, relative to the white-owned ventures in which minority-oriented VC funds invest. Here again our findings are mixed. While the MBEs do indeed receive smaller VC investments than white-owned portfolio firms, holding constant year of investment, industry, syndication and similar traits, it is also true that MBEs receive larger investments, on average, from new-generation funds than they do when funded by the old-generation VC funds. Recall, as well, our earlier finding that public pension funds and funds of funds prefer to invest in minority-oriented VC funds holding portfolios of firms of diverse racial ownership.

The clear implication of this fact is that funds actively investing in both white-owned and MBE portfolio firms are precisely the funds most responsible for increasing the total capital resources which minority-oriented VC funds have available to invest in their portfolio firms. The fact that the pie is expanding suggests that more – rather than less – funding is most likely available for MBEs in this era of expanding new-generation fund presence. The reality of MBEs receiving smaller average equity investments than their white-firm counterparts is consistent with the steadily rising average investment sizes MBEs have been receiving from their VC funders over the decade 1995 through year end 2004. Rising investment size, furthermore, is coexisting with growth in the average number of new equity investments in MBEs being made annually by minority-oriented VC funds.

This growth in VC funding availability and increasing investment size among MBE venture capital recipients is certainly not being helped by the declining incidence of syndication of investments funded by the minority-oriented VC funds. The new-generation funds in particular are less actively involved in syndicating their VC investments, relative to the old generation of minority-oriented VC funds. Precise statistics are presented below to illuminate key differences in VC investing patterns in MBEs versus white-owned portfolio firms, as well as differences between old-and new-generation minority-oriented VC funds.

Tables 11 and 12 provide measures of central tendency first for MBE portfolio firms only and the funds investing in these firms, and then for white-owned portfolio firms and their MBE counterparts. Our objective is to highlight racial differences regarding 1) investment size, 2) industry distribution of portfolio firms, 3) patterns in syndication and other VC fund traits, and 4) investment timing, comparing how MBEs – as opposed to white-owned portfolio firms— differ regarding the above. Are VC-fund investments in MBEs somehow different than equity investments in white-owned firms and, if so, exactly how do they differ?

In fact, these two groups of firms and the traits of the minority-oriented funds providing them with venture capital are strikingly different. Regarding fund strategy, investments in MBEs, according to the group mean differences summarized in table 12, are more likely to be syndicated (relative to white-owned portfolio firms), smaller in terms of dollar amount invested, less likely to be recipients of activist GP intervention in their management decisions making, and larger numbers of MBEs have been funded (10.3) per fund general partner, in comparison to white-owned portfolio firms (8.6). These findings are broadly consistent with the results of regression analysis exercises discussed above.

Regarding other traits, MBEs are heavily concentrated in communications and under represented in hi-tech fields. Note, however, that white-owned firms are more likely than MBEs to be found in the portfolios of VC funds investing actively in old-economy lines of business (table 12). The nonminority firms, as expected, are over represented among investments initiated by the VC funds during the peak investing years 1999 and 2000, and they are disproportionately funded by new-generation funds.

Finally, it is noteworthy that average realized IRR values for the white portfolio firms (-0.30) were lower than the corresponding IRRs of the MBEs. Note that the negative mean IRR values do not imply that the VC investing activities of the minority-oriented funds under consideration were unprofitable.

IRR values, although universally used to measure returns generated by VC funds on their realized investments, are quirky measures of returns. Median IRR values are flawed as well but, interestingly, a comparison of median IRRs for the firm groups described in table 12 indicates positive values overall for realized MBE investments, negative values for white-owned ventures, and an aggregate median value of -.01 for all 303 realized investments of the combined groups. Idiosyncratic traits of IRR return measures are further discussed in Bates and Bradford, 2003.

Table 11. Minority Firm Summary Statistics, Investments Realized through Year end 2006

Variable:	Mean	Median
IRR-all investments (equally weighted)	-0.19	0.00
Old-generation fund	0.91	1.00
Log of investment	12.68	12.68
Syndicated	0.92	1.00
High tech	0.20	0.18
Communications	0.47	0.42
Medical services	0.03	0.00
Old economy	0.17	0.16
Year of investment, 1999 or 2000	0.25	0.00
Investments Per GP	10.26	7.67
Activism	0.84	1.00
N= 273		

Table 12. MBE versus Nonminority Means Comparisons (Investments Realized through Year end 2006)

Variable:	Mean: white- owned firms only	Mean: MBEs only
IRR-all investments (equally weighted)	-0.30	-0.19
Old-generation fund	0.60	0.91
Log of investment	14.5	12.7
Syndicated	0.76	0.92
High tech	0.24	0.20
Communications	0.24	0.47
Medical services	0.03	0.03
Old economy	0.25	0.17
Year of investment, 1999 or 2000	0.40	0.25
Investments Per GP	8.6	10.3
Activism	0.87	.84
N	30	273

F. Robustness Tests

Our final task regarding our analysis of the viability of the minority-oriented venture-capital industry entails conducting several statistical tests to establish the robustness of our findings concerning VC-fund strategies and portfolio company traits associated with stronger (and weaker) financial performance, measured by IRR values of their realized investments. We have conducted a variety of these tests, which entail estimating variants of the table 6 regression analysis explaining variance in IRR values; (see, as well, Jackson et al. (forthcoming) for detailed discussion of the robustness of our regression model for explaining IRR values of realized investments made by minority-oriented VC funds.

The regression exercise summarized in table 13 entails analyzing relationships between the IRR values of 273 realized investments in MBEs and fund and portfolio firm traits; white-owned portfolio firms are excluded. We are replicating the regression analysis summarized in table 6, but solely for MBE portfolio firms. Regression findings identify the firm traits and VC-fund strategies that predict high returns on investment in MBEs, and these include 1) GP activism, 2) not initiating new investments in the peak funding years of 1999 and 2000, 3) investments made by new-generation funds, 4) larger numbers of investments per GP, and 5) investments in portfolio firms operating in the medical services industry (table 13). Two findings particularly stand out:

1) new-generation funds clearly earn higher returns on their investments in MBEs than old-generation funds;

2) there is no penalty attached to syndicated investments (table 13). Earlier regression findings (table 6) revealed lower returns on syndicated investments, other factors being equal. Furthermore, previously reported regression findings had not established the positive relationship demonstrated in table 13 between new-generation-fund investments and higher IRRs on realized VC investments in MBE portfolio companies. Since future developments in the trajectory of the minority-oriented VC industry sector appear to be driven largely by new-generation funds, their demonstrated ability to invest successfully in MBEs is an important finding. We conclude that the table 13—and various other regression analyses – regression exercise is producing consistent outcomes, which is the defining characteristic of a robust statistical analysis.

Table 13. GLS Random Effects Regression Model Explaining Relationships between IRR Values of Realized Investments and Traits of VC Funds and their Minority-Owned Portfolio Firms

Variable	Coefficient	T-ratio
Constant	-0.42	-0.94
Old-generation fund	-0.33**	-4.12
Log of investment	0.02	0.93
Syndicated	-0.08	-0.79
High tech	-0.24	-0.77
Communications	-0.06	-0.27
Medical services	1.45*	2.52
Old economy	0.04	0.13
Year of investment, 1999 or 2000	-0.49**	-8.82
Investments Per GP	0.03**	4.54
Activism	0.24**	3.59
N= 273		
Adj-R2	0.13	
F-statistic	21.24**	

** significant at the one percent level or better .
* significant at the 5 percent level or better.
Robust standard errors are utilized.

III. CONCLUSION

Has high-tech investing been particularly profitable for the minority-oriented VC funds? The answer is no. Has investing in portfolio companies owned by whites been particularly profitable? Once again, the answer is no. What profiles and strategies typify the more successful, as opposed to the less successful minority VC funds? Higher IRR values are associated with 1) investing in MBEs, 2) activism in assisting portfolio companies on the part of the VC fund general partners, and 3) a larger number of VC investments per fund general partner. It is noteworthy that all of these traits linked to higher returns on VC investments represent investing strategies employed at the discretion of the individual VC funds. Lower IRR values are associated with 1) making investments in white-owned firms, 2) being an older VC fund, 3) participating in syndicated investments, and 4) top-of-the-cycle investing (making investments initially funded in either 1999 or 2000).

Our findings validate the underserved minority market hypothesis: investing in MBEs, other factors being the same, generates higher returns for the minority VC funds than investments in nonminority-owned ventures. In English, this means that investments of the same dollar amount, initiated in the same time period, by minority-oriented VC funds using identical strategies regarding such factors as syndication, investment by industry, GP activism with portfolio companies, and the like, produced higher IRR values if the portfolio company was minority owned and lower values if the company was white owned.

We attribute the generally declining financial returns typifying the minority-oriented VC funds in recent years to five factors, three of which reflect the tendency of these funds to emulate mainstream VC industry investing practices. First, cooperation among funds in the form of syndicated investing has declined, a trend mirroring mainstream investing practices. We credit subsequent declining returns to the fact that minority VC funds are increasingly keeping their most promising investments entirely for themselves, while syndicating the less promising deals in order to spread the risk of a poor ultimate outcome for these deals. Second, the increasing frequency of investments in white-owned portfolio companies—rather than MBEs – has clearly depressed realized investment returns. Investing in hi-tech companies, third, is another factor tending to lower returns on realized equity investments in portfolio companies.

Investments initially funded in the years 1999 or 2000 by minority-oriented funds—investing at the very top of the VC industry's boom/bust cycle – were the fourth cause of low realized returns on VC investments; in comparison, investments initiated before or after 1999 and 2000 were much more successful. Investing heavily at the top of a boom/bust cycle, while certainly a negative, is most likely a transitory phenomenon rather than a strategic choice likely to indicate enduring poor financial returns on the equity investments made by the minority-oriented VC funds. Fund vintage, finally, shaped investing returns, a finding that suggests a brighter future for the minority-oriented VC fund sector. The older funds were the ones most often producing low returns on realized equity investments, holding other factors constant, while the newer-generation funds – those most directly shaping the future trajectory – were the better performers. These newer VC funds are typically run by GPs possessing work experience in investment banking prior to launching their venture capital funds, while GPs of older funds rarely possessed such mainstream work experience. Our findings suggest that having prior work experience in investment banking conveyed investing advantages.

The question "why would these VC funds in the 21st century increasingly invest outside of their traditional minority market niche?" is closely linked to the investing preferences of the institutional investors that provide the funding for the venture capital industry. Major institutional investors like pension funds seek high financial returns when they invest in VC funds. When they contemplate investing into minority-oriented VC funds, they seek to cherry-pick the winners, investing only in the subset of minority funds poised to generate above-average returns for their institutional investors. In the process of picking and choosing those funds potentially offering the highest investment returns, the institutional investors effectively shape the trajectory of the minority VC industry subsector. The winners—flush with funding — rapidly achieve growing prominence in the MBE equity investing realm; the losers—smaller in resources available for investing—lose relative position within the minority VC fund universe.

Our findings and those of other researchers indicate that the dominant institutional investors providing funding to the minority-oriented VC funds have systematically tended to invest in the less profitable VC funds, including those investing most actively in hi-tech and white-owned portfolio companies. Importantly, however, the investing practices of these institutional capital sources are self-correcting over time precisely because their funding decisions are driven largely by their search for above-average returns. We therefore see this institutional investor set of preferences as a short-term phenomenon, with future funding flowing increasingly to the minority-oriented VC funds pursuing the equity investing strategies most clearly identified with generating high returns on their VC investments; minority-owned business ventures provide those higher returns.

One fact is clear: absent generating high competitive returns on their equity investments in small business ventures, minority-oriented VC funds will not retain their access in the future to major institutional sources of funding such as public pension funds. Further, those individual VC funds earning high competitive returns on their VC investments will enjoy continuing access to institutional capital sources in the future, and the funds producing uncompetitive low returns will be denied such access. The future of the minority-oriented VC funds is thus shaped largely by how successfully they generate high returns on their realized equity investments in small businesses.

Scholarly studies have repeatedly demonstrated that minority-owned business enterprises, particularly those owned by African Americans and Hispanics, have less access to debt and equity capital than similarly situated white-owned firms. When MBEs experience restricted access to equity capital markets, this market segment is being underserved. Indeed, minority-oriented equity-investing venture capital funds exist today largely due to the absence of mainstream VC-fund participation in this market segment. Two direct empirical tests for the presence or absence of restricted MBE access to equity capital have been discussed in this report, the first of which entails comparing the financial performance of VC funds specializing in investing in MBEs, to the outcomes of mainstream VC funds of the same vintage that do not target their investments to MBEs (Bates and Bradford, 2008a). An alternative test of the underserved market hypothesis requires collecting data on all realized VC investments made by a group of funds over a specific time period, where some of these funds actively made VC investments in both MBE- and nonminority-owned small businesses. The underserved market hypothesis is supported if the observed investment returns forthcoming from realized VC investments in MBEs exceeded returns from investments in the non-MBE ventures. Results of this alternative test – documenting higher financial returns forthcoming from VC investments in MBEs—provide statistically significant support for the underserved market hypothesis. This suggests that minority-oriented VC funds are viable and serve as a important source of equity capital for MBEs. This is the major single finding of this research report.

Other major findings in this report related to the two following research questions. First, does diversifying outside the underserved minority market niche increase or decrease the quality of the management support services received by MBEs? And, second, does the amount of equity capital that minority-oriented VC funds provide to their portfolio of minority-owned small businesses decrease when they diversify outside the underserved minority market niche? Our findings suggest that the answers to both of these questions are nuanced. We conclude that general partner activist involvement in the management of its portfolio companies impacts MBEs in diverse ways. The more activist GPs would undoubtedly benefit more minority-owned portfolio companies if they chose to invest in fewer white-owned business ventures. However, the countervailing fact is that VC funds entirely oriented toward MBE investing are less likely than their counterparts to intervene as actively in day-to-day management decision making with their portfolio firms. Thus, increasing the number of minority-oriented VC funds that diversify into non-MBE investing may result in an overall increase of GP involvement with MBEs. Similarly, our findings indicate, on balance, that investing in nonminority ventures does not reduce the supply of venture capital funding available to minority-owned firms.

A. Additional Research Topics

Several areas for additional research are suggested by the findings of this report. First, are VC-fund investments in MBEs somehow different than equity investments in white-owned firms and, if so, exactly how do they differ? Our findings suggest that, in fact, these racially-defined groups of portfolio firms—and the traits of the minority-oriented funds providing them with venture capital—are strikingly different. Regarding fund strategy, for example investments in MBEs are more likely to be syndicated (relative to white-owned portfolio firms), smaller in terms of dollar amount invested, less likely to be recipients of activist GP intervention in their management decision making, and larger numbers of MBEs are funded per fund general partner, in comparison to white-owned portfolio firms. These findings suggest that a better understanding of these differences, especially the relative importance of syndicating and networking among MBEs, is a fruitful area for future research.

B. Public Policy

Our results provide additional documentation of the existence of underserved markets in the realm of MBE financing, indicating that access to equity capital among MBEs is still a challenge. Policies to support minority-oriented VC funds may be capable of alleviating this market failure, thus enhancing the competitiveness of MBEs specifically, while enhancing, as well, the overall competitiveness of the nation's private sector.

According to the Kauffman Index of Entrepreneurial Activity, a leading indicator of new business creation trends in the U.S. economy, minority owners made up 24 percent of all new entrepreneurs in the U.S. in 1996, but the minority share by 2010 had risen to 40 percent. A related relevant fact is that the majority of all children in the U.S. under the age of four in 2010 are minorities, which clarifies why the U.S. about three decades from now will be a nation where non-Hispanic whites make up under half of the total population.

"Unless we unleash the potential of the minority population" note Greenhalgh and Lowrey, "the past success of the U.S....cannot be sustained in the coming decades" (2011, p. 16). Researchers to date have emphasized the importance of MBEs as creators of jobs in minority communities, an important point.

Going forward, however, MBEs must be seen as vitally important creators of economic growth and new employment opportunities not simply for minority communities but for the nation as a whole.

APPENDIX A. DATABASE DESCRIBING MBE-ORIENTED VC FUNDS AND THEIR EQUITY INVESTMENTS IN SMALL BUSINESSES

The VC fund database analyzed in this study was constructed by surveying NAIC member funds at three points in time – 2001, 2004, and 2007. In our 2004 and 2007 surveys, several funds responding to an earlier survey did not respond, while several not responding to an earlier survey did respond to later ones.

To ensure adequate representation of young funds in our final sample, we permitted funds starting between 2001 and 2003 to be included in our 2004 survey of eligible NAIC member funds. Member firms were pre-surveyed again in 2004 to identify those oriented toward investing equity capital in minority business enterprises.

Further descriptions of this VC-fund database are available in Jackson et al. (forthcoming).

APPENDIX B. VARIABLE DEFINITIONS

Dependent Variables

1. Tables 6, 8, 13 and 14:
IRR: The internal rate of return (IRR) for the project is the discount rate at which the present values of all of the investment's cash flows sum to zero.
2. Tables 9 and 10: Activism is an indicator variable equal to one if assistance is provided by the VC fund general partners in the day-to-day operations of its portfolio firms, and zero otherwise.

Explanatory Variables

Precise variable definitions are spelled out in Bates and Bradford (2008b).

REFERENCES

Admati, A., and P. Pfleiderer. (1994). Robust financial contracting and the role of venture capitalists. *Journal of Finance*, 49, 371-402.

Bates, T. (1997a). *Race, Self Employment, and Upward Mobility.* Baltimore: Johns Hopkins University Press.

Bates, T. (1997b). The Minority Enterprise Small Business Investment Company program. *Urban Affairs Review.* 32: 683-703.

Bates, T., and W. Bradford. (2009). The impact of institutional sources of capital upon the minority-oriented venture capital industry. *Small Business Economics.* 33: 481-92.

Bates, T., and W. Bradford. (2008a). Venture capital investment in minority business. *Journal of Money, Credit, and Banking*, 40: 489-504.

Bates, T., and W. Bradford. (2008b). *Evaluating the Performance of the Minority-Oriented Venture Capital Industry.* Kansas City: E.M. Kauffman Foundation.

Bates, T., and W. Bradford. (2003). *Minorities and Venture Capital*, E.M. Kauffman Foundation, Kansas City, MO.

Bates, T., and W. Bradford. (1992). Factors affecting new firm success and their use in venture capital financing. *The Journal of Small Business Finance.* 2: 23-38.

Bates, T., W. Bradford, and J. Rubin. (2006). The viability of the minority-oriented venture-capital industry under alternative financing arrangements. *Economic Development Quarterly, 20:178-91.*

Boston, T., and C. Ross. (1997). Location preferences of successful African American- owned businesses in Atlanta. In T. Boston and C. Ross (eds.). *The inner city.* New Brunswick: Transaction Publishers.

Brander, J., R. Amit, and W. Antweiler. (2002). Venture capital syndication: Improved venture selection vs. the value-added hypothesis. *Journal of Economics and Management Strategy,* 11, 423-451.

Brophy, D. (1997). Financing the growth of entrepreneurial firms, in P. Sexton and R. Smilor, (eds). *Entrepreneurship 2000.* (Chicago: Upstart).

Carter, D., and R. Wilson. (1992). *Minorities in higher education.* Washington, D.C.: American Council on Higher Education.

Cavalluzzo, K., and J. Wolken. (2005). Small business loan turndowns, personal wealth and discrimination. *Journal of Business.* 78: 2153-78.

Chen, P., G. Baierl, and P. Kaplan. (2002). Venture capital and its role in strategic asset allocation. *Journal of Portfolio Management,* 28: 83-89.

Cochrane, J. (2005). The risk and return of venture capital. *Journal of Financial Economics,* 75:3-52.

Gompers, P., Lerner, J., 1999. The Venture Capital Cycle, MIT Press, Cambridge, MA.

Green, P., and M. Owen. (2004). Race and ethnicity. In William Gartner et al., (Eds.), *Handbook of entrepreneurial dynamics.* Thousand Oaks, CA: Sage.

Greenhalgh, L., and J. Lowrey. (2011). *Minority Business Success: Refocusing On the American Dream.* Stanford, CA: Stanford University Press.

Harvey, W. (2003). *Minorities in higher education, 2002-2003.* Washington, D.C.: American Council on Higher Education.

Hellmann, T., and M. Puri. (2002). Venture capital and the professionalization of start-up firms: Empirical evidence. *Journal of Finance,* 57, 169-197.

Jackson, W., T. Bates, and W. Bradford. (forthcoming). Does venture capitalist activism improve investment performance? *Journal of Business Venturing.*

Kaplan, S., and P. Stromberg. (2004). Characteristics, contracts, and actions: Evidence from venture capitalist analyses. *Journal of Finance,* 59, 2177–210.

Kaplan, S., and A. Schoar. (2005). Private equity performance: Returns, persistence and capital flows, *Journal of Finance* 60: 1971-2003.

Ljungqvist, A., and M. Richardson. (2004). The cash flow, return and risk characteristics of private equity. National Bureau of Economic Research, Working Paper No. 9454.

Meyer, R., D. Butler, E. Caragannis, and R. Radovich. (1995). *The 1999 National Census of Early Stage Venture Capital Financing*. Albuquerque: Orion.

Norton, E., and B. Tenenbaum. (1993). Specialization versus diversification as a venture capital investment strategy. *Journal of Business Venturing*, 8: 431-42.

Sah, R., and Stiglitz, J. (1986). The architecture of economic systems: Hierarchies and polyarchies. *American Economic Review*, 76, 716-727.

Sapienza, H. (1992). When do venture capitalists add value? *Journal of Business Venturing*, 7: 9- 27.

U.S. Bureau of the Census, Survey of Business Owners, (2002). (released in 2006) – downloaded from the website of the Bureau of the Census on November 5, 2010.

INDEX

D

E

F